**Other books written
By Dan LaFave:**

"Shadow Of The Ghost Hunter"

THE SUPERNATURAL, TEXAS, AND THE OLD WEST

....THE MYSTERIOUS, REAL HAUNTING PARANORMAL WORLD OF GHOSTS

Dan LaFave

3

The Supernatural, Texas, And The Old West.... The Mysterious Real Haunting Paranormal World Of Ghosts

2nd Edition
Copyright © 2013
By Dan LaFave
Published in the United States of America
ALL RIGHTS RESERVED
ISBN-13: 978-1484826218
ISBN-10: 1484826213
Harlingen, Texas

Library Of Congress Control Number: 2013901925

Table Of Contents

Foreword

The wild west of old Texas and the surrounding other states in the Southwest and South were truly at one time a rough, hard enduring place for many to live their lives. So many people with a dream of pursuit of land, liberty, and what they thought would be freedom came to this very unforgiving, sometimes brutal frontier landscape of which a lot at the time was under the control of Mexican authority and government.

These pioneering people and the forefathers of Texas history came with the dream of finding land and building their life stories and legacies with their hard work, sweat, blood, and tears in their extreme dedication for what they sought as to a new life as so many of them in those days described it. What many of these people found, however, upon their travels from the more modern civilized Northeast regions of the developing United States was a very rough, harsh, and untamed land and alien world that upon looking at the first time showed that these dreams were possible, but at the same time would be brutal. So many people died by both natural but also very violent means at much younger than expected ages. For many, their lives were decided one day in a single violent instant by the knife, bullet, or rope.

In this exciting book, I strive to take the interested reader to various real confirmed haunting locations that I have seen, experienced, and witnessed as to true ghostly Texas past.....to take the reader into a mysterious uncharted and sometimes extremely scary existing ghostly world that is sure to grab the attention of the modern thinking mind. To put the reader or avid paranormal enthusiast in another place set aside from the realities of the world we live in. To make a person think that what they think may be a very normal world, may not exactly be what it appears......especially when it comes to the real ghostly world. Also the curiosity of why real ghosts possibly dwell within these Texas and other Wild West locations.

You see, an experienced paranormal investigator/researcher such as myself and others have seen and witnessed many sometimes unnatural shocking things over the years in exploring this mysterious world. These things can be frightening to some people because they are hard to imagine or comprehend. Some people do not believe in ghosts. The skeptical people will always be there because of the fact that they have not had an extreme ghostly event occur to them. Sometimes it is just a matter of time. My life for a long time has been about researching very real ghostly paranormal or supernatural activity in certain locations. I dwell within the real ghostly haunting stories that many people tell. The best ghost story is the one that is lived. Come take a walk as to exploring and learning this exciting ghostly haunted world to experience what we have seen.

~ Dan LaFave

Prologue

It was approximately 8 pm; the same time that I, my wife Connie, and our paranormal team/group Graveyard Shift Paranormal Investigations usually started our many controlled detailed investigations. There was no moon that night. We had traveled nearly 4 hours this day on the highway to this mysterious historic forgotten Texas ghost town called Helena, Texas. This was a place that someone could drive past quite easily without even noticing because of how it has shrunk over time. Once we gathered and distributed our paranormal equipment, both myself, my wife Connie, and one of our fellow paranormal researchers and associates Harvey Martinez headed over to investigate one of the old buildings with reported high paranormal activity within from several very reliable and credible sources.

This historic building was at one time the old Masonic Lodge (where also the KGC – Knights of the Golden Circle, a notorious group, used to hang out in the 1800's). It is believed by some that Helena might have been one of the KGC's main secret meeting areas as to planning out things for The Civil War. The old dated Masonic order/charter is still posted on the wall to view. As we entered and started our paranormal investigation around 9 pm that night within the Masonic Lodge, we all started to feel extreme things around us in which we knew we were not alone. We were standing there in the extreme darkness trying to get our eyes to adjust looking at things when suddenly the environment around us began to change. We could feel it. We knew that we were no longer alone and that we were indeed within someone else's domain, possibly that we stepped into another time in history.

What was it? We could feel the hair on our arms, necks, and heads suddenly stand up. There suddenly was an extreme feeling of electricity and energy in the dark large room around us. That very strange feeling we experienced sometimes in certain paranormal environments when something very unnatural and wild was about to occur. That feeling that puts even seasoned paranormal investigators/researchers on edge at times. A soulful feeling was felt where even though there were three of us in that very dim and spooky room, we all suddenly felt alone.

In that total darkness while all three of us were standing very still with the front door entirely closed, we suddenly very loudly and clearly could hear movement and footsteps coming towards us from the back area. The personal feeling was as if something unseen was stalking and watching us. Was it an animal? No, it quite clearly was not. We all looked towards that area. Suddenly, we got the answer we were looking for when a large rock picked up off the floor by something was thrown very hard against the deteriorating wood ceiling structure right above our heads to then land and bounce at our feet. In a second, we all looked up first trying to focus our eyes to the rattling vibrating ceiling structure above and then to the large cement rock laying now at our feet. We all could feel and sense it then with an alarming sense.......the unseen.....when one of us gasped loudly "Oh God!"

Chapter 1: Ghostly Texas Haunts

Harlingen, Texas

Families were stricken with diseases that many of us find very common now, but in those days of long ago were very fast acting and quite deadly in the old West. It is hard to imagine that a simple cold or infection from a simple wound could have killed a person, but it happened because of the lack of proper antibiotics and medicines which are common now. In looking at and examining old historical documents in various places around Texas, I found that there was indeed a hidden past of Texas and the Old West that showed that many people did indeed die from many natural ordinary causes as well as violent ones. Much of this information was never shown in history books in school.

With that, I asked myself why has some of this information been left out or omitted.

In walking around Texas historical cemeteries, I have seen through observation and research in various areas around Texas that there were times where not talked about epidemics of tuberculosis, flu, polio, and other various respiratory ailments struck inflicted communities and affected people of all ages sometimes in a rapid and sweeping manner where the populations died. Some of these communities were once prosperous only to die and fade away over time for various reasons. I have walked through historic towns stepping back in history and looking for clues of these frontier people and their ghosts that still might possibly linger and lurk in the modern existence we live in now waiting and wanting to tell their story. .

In doing research of old Texas cemeteries and towns, and really taking the time to pay close attention to what people encountered in those days, a serious paranormal investigator and researcher can gain quite a lot of knowledge through observation as to why paranormal activity might be occurring in places on high levels and not occurring in other places. When a paranormal researcher is contacted by someone claiming that there is a form of ghostly paranormal activity occurring in a various location, a serious paranormal researcher not only looks at what presently stands in front of either himself or herself, but rather of what once stood in this location possibly hundreds of years ago.

Walking amongst the old cemetery markers and gravesites, I have gained a lot of perspective from many years of looking at and researching real ghosts and paranormal activity of old Texas and the Wild West. I have learned through talking with various other Texas historians at times and doing my own research of locations, that there was a lot more than initially met the eye on why some of this real confirmed paranormal activity might actually be occurring in locations.

I found that parts of old Texas were actually very brutal in which a person did not know if they were going to either live or die the next day. There were several old western gangs that rode the trails of Texas along with various bandits and also violent Indian attacks that took place. There were sections of Texas that people moved to with the hopes of developing and creating a new life only to instead encounter a very harsh untamed land that was unwilling to succumb to being tamed as to modern civilization.

You see, it again was a very hard time for many with numerous things occurring in old Texas history like battles, skirmishes with bandits or Indians, or run-ins with the developing law structure which a lot of times were just as ruthless as the criminals that they claimed to be protecting the settlers from. You have most likely heard about the legends of both lawmen and other gunslinger or what we call outlaw names alike......Wyatt Earp, Bat Masterson, Doc Holliday, Jesse James, Billy The Kid, Pat Garrett, Geronimo, Belle Starr, Butch Cassidy and The Sundance Kid, John Wesley Hardin, Doolin-Dawton Gang, John Kinney Gang, and many others.

There were many names because again this was a very ruthless land during those times. For many, the simple law or rule was the knife, gun, or hangman's rope. Sometimes people were caught right in the middle of things like this with nothing to do but try to hang on. I can imagine that a lot of these people probably wondered what they had gotten themselves into as to coming to this untamed and brutal land that is now the great state of Texas. Many people faced extreme brutality in the form of random uncontrolled lynching's consisting of random shootings, hangings, and other very severe forms of torture.

I was born and raised in Texas and thus this is how I came to researching and exploring Texas the way that I do as a very serious paranormal investigator/researcher and part-time historian. I personally feel that in a way I was drawn into this world and chosen for this journey of new discovery and exploration of this mysterious existence. I believe after many years that real paranormal/supernatural activity and history does mix a lot of times in certain locations for various unknown reasons still to be found out.

I did not go looking for the paranormal/supernatural many years ago, it seems that this intriguing world reached out and found me somehow and presented itself. In looking at all of this over many years of paranormal investigative research and wondering why various Texas and other old West frontier locations are either haunted or contain a degree or level of ghostly paranormal activity, I have found that trying to put all the pieces of the paranormal puzzle together do indeed show a very wild, wild ghostly Texas that is indeed very interesting as to both history and its ghostly past.

During my time investigating and researching Texas and other locations in other states around Texas as to the supernatural, I realized that I truly had some remarkable very real ghostly paranormal experiences in locations that I should share. During discussions with the public (book signings, paranormal events, seminars, and rotary club meetings), I have talked about some of these experiences where people looked back at me very wide-eyed with deep interest and fascination. Some of these discussions could easily go two hours where I would not even cover the basis of everything I have encountered with the paranormal/supernatural within historic locations around Texas and other locations. You see, a paranormal researcher over time encounters quite a lot of really compelling sometimes quite disturbing or scary paranormal moments that sometimes are just from personal experience or might possibly be recorded and confirmed in some other instrumental capacity.

The moments of personal paranormal experience by surprise are the most easily remembered however in that those moments are truly engrained in the brain and recollected and remembered over time. Most people who have never done what a serious paranormal investigator/researcher has done over time, really have no true idea of what is involved or experienced. It is very easy to put a ghost story into words, but a total other experience to live that ghost story in a very real way. An experienced paranormal researcher on one hand is looking for very good compelling confirmed and correlated ghostly paranormal activity, but soon realizes that those moments are truly hard to capture by instruments and other witness account. The shock and surprise when things are seen, heard, or experienced in other ways personally however are amazing, and there really are no substitutes to a true life ghost story that is relived over and over in a person's memory and mind.

I as a serious paranormal researcher have encountered every form of paranormal activity there is over many years and surprisingly a lot of this occurs at strange surprising moments when least expected in places that an investigator may not necessarily comprehend it to occur. There are some paranormal places out there that a paranormal researcher easily remembers for the extreme ghostly experience. This ghostly world is very real even though some skeptics will try to rationalize that it is all naturally occurring and possibly the imagination or hallucination of the people investigating the phenomena. As I have always said, the non-believers are skeptics usually because they have never had a real extreme paranormal/supernatural event occur personally to them. The believers believe as to what they have personally experienced beyond a reason of doubt, not by what someone else has told them about this ghostly world.

In Texas, there is a lot of old western history of brutality and stories that make the hair rise up on end in hearing those stories. Two hundred years ago, Texas and the states around Texas were a very hard place to live. People moved from the Northeast regions as to finding land and creating a new life. They however never suspected to run into the types of things that were found upon getting to Texas and finding out just how rugged this new land was. In many locations of Texas, there virtually was no sign of law and justice was literally carried out by lynching in the form of hanging or shooting. A person's life was hanging at the end of a thread so to speak and many people did not live long lives in those days for certain reasons related to this.

In starting to research Texas years ago and travel to places, I soon realized that the old Texas history was screaming to be heard. That the ghosts from that past are simply waiting to be heard. I have found in many locations around Texas, that this ghostly and haunted past is really there and in the strangest unknown places a person would ever imagine. You see, many people don't know or forget over time how certain locations looked or what was there before. There are many ghost towns in Texas that simply evaporated and disappeared for various reasons, sometimes created from very brutal circumstances that stemmed from personal vengeance or greed towards land or money. I have found that there is a lot to be discovered still with the paranormal ghostly world in Texas and the states around Texas. I have found that the ghosts all have a tale to tell as to these places. Every place seems to have a hidden story to tell, and the ghosts of the past possibly are just waiting for someone in the modern world to take the time to listen to what they have to say or show. This may sound funny or strange in the way I present this information here, but any serious paranormal investigator/researcher or person with an avid fascination towards the paranormal/supernatural world knows exactly what I mean when I state it like this. We over time forget how places were. We a lot of times neglect and permanently erase the history of the past for modern reasons of development. Many cities and locations change a lot in say just 30 years......imagine what that change involves over a 200 year period?

Researching the paranormal ghostly world can be very interesting, but at the same time can be quite scary. Many people label what we do as investigators to simply be crazy in a sense of the word. Who do you know who goes into very old, abandoned, forgotten, sometimes very haunted locations in complete darkness searching for ghostly things to happen? I can say that there are not many of us that seriously do this on the level that we do it. There are groups that do this as a hobby and there are teams that do this for much more as to research reasons.....and that is to make possible contact and go to the next level as to new discovery in the ghostly paranormal world. We want to try to answer the real who, what, where, when, and how as to this world. In researching the paranormal ghostly world after many years now, we strive for much more.....and that is not just to confirm if a place/location has paranormal activity in it, but instead we go to locations to really bring out existing paranormal activity on much higher levels so that we can observe and try to document it more. We go to make contact.....or as some will say, talk with the dead. Again, many people will say that we are crazy or out of our mind in wanting to do this. Some will ask why we do this. Some will ask what our purpose is. Many of us come from very professional lifestyles and professions. Some of us again do this in a hobby perspective just to see what they will find, while others such as ourselves do it with much more commitment looking for much more in trying to find the answers as to why paranormal/supernatural activity is occurring at times in certain locations and not other locations. I can say however on the other hand that we are actually very educated, logical, rational, intelligent researchers that are simply doing what we like to do best --- seek the real ghostly paranormal truth. I can also say personally from years of investigating and researching many very real paranormal/supernatural locations throughout Texas, that this state has a lot to offer in this area with so much more new discovery to be made. I can also say that sometimes – yes, some of these what I regard as real confirmed haunted locations across Texas can be quite scary and unnerving........if that is what you are truly looking for. It is exciting to say the least and is a real adrenaline feeling when extreme paranormal activity occurs. There is no way to truly explain that feeling, a person just has to go out.......and does it.

Chapter 2: Yorktown Hospital
(Yorktown, Texas)

Photo By: Dan LaFave

It seems there is some old abandoned hospital somewhere written about in just about every paranormal book by someone. This is very true, there probably is. There, however, are no hospitals out there in my opinion just like Yorktown, Hospital which is located in small Yorktown, Texas approximately 75 miles from San Antonio, Texas. When I state this, it is proven fact that there are indeed some very sinister paranormal and supernatural happenings occurring within the confines of this hospital.

Now, I, my Connie, and our paranormal team Graveyard Shift Paranormal Investigations have been involved with this hospital a lot since it was originally discovered and confirmed in 2008 to have sometimes extreme paranormal/supernatural activity occurring at times to people. When I say people, am talking about all sorts of people.....ranging from local ordinary citizens of Yorktown, past security guards of the grounds, people doing construction or maintenance within the building, people taking tours of the hospital during the day, and various reputable paranormal teams or organizations over time. Years back, I actually met and am very good personal friends with the owner of Yorktown Hospital, Phil Ross (an attorney), and also his partner Jo Ann Rivera (the owner of Black Swan Inn in San Antonio, Texas – which is another very haunted location I have investigated and will discuss in another later chapter).

While I and my wife Connie were lead paranormal investigators/researchers on another reputable Texas paranormal team SAPN (San Antonio Paranormal Network/TAPS Family Member Team), we helped introduce and open Yorktown Hospital to the public as to the paranormal activity taking within it. The owner, Phil Ross, had come across purchasing the hospital through business dealings and had also heard of the rumored paranormal activity happenings within the hospital. Both he and his partner Jo Ann and others soon discovered that there were indeed very strange unexplainable things happening within this hospital having to do with the supernatural. In September 2008, both myself, my wife Connie, the founding members of SAPN (Robert and Michelle Hernandez), other members of that team, along with the owner Phil Ross, Jo Ann Rivera, Angelka Rogers, and Mike Hanson all got together to help and hold a paranormal investigation with about 30 other paranormal enthusiasts from around the state of Texas for the first time at Yorktown Hospital in that capacity to see what everyone might find and discover. Even though everyone had a lot of fun investigating together and it was very interesting as to some paranormal very interesting things (audio, video, and picture) found that night, there really were too many people present at the time to have a real controlled paranormal investigation on finding really good paranormal evidence.

In July 2009 about 9 months later, myself and my wife Connie decided to do something really special as to the paranormal at Yorktown Hospital. We decided and started planning to do an hour and half long paranormal documentary (the first at Yorktown Hospital) of an all night very controlled paranormal investigation by our group within Yorktown Hospital with a full DVR static camera setup, and 4 of us investigating throughout the night to see what could be found and discovered that might be paranormal in nature.

Photo By: Dan LaFave

The nightly investigation ran from 8 pm to approximately 5 am in the morning, and was very eventful as to very real paranormal/supernatural things occurring.

Photo By: Dan LaFave

When a person walks the hallways of Yorktown Hospital even during the day, you really feel something eerie about the location. There are so many shadows within this old hospital that seem to reach out to you at times. A person feels themselves constantly turning around and looking. There are also times of dread that seem to overtake people. The main thing is that you cannot place exactly where all the eeriness feeling is coming, but when you are alone.......you simply don't want to be alone in that old hospital too long. Many people get a nauseous feeling that comes on very quickly as well walking the hallways. Those people go outside, and within a few minutes are fine again.

Photo By: Dan LaFave

To say that you are being watched is simply not enough. To say that something is maybe there waiting and lurking to do something to you is more like it. I never really ever had that feeling before that something was trying to prey upon me until this July 2009 investigation that we did. I personally have been in working hospitals and also other large non-working abandoned hospitals in my lifetime, and never have I had such a feeling that I sometimes have had walking the hallways and basement of Yorktown Hospital.

It is not easy for a seasoned paranormal investigator/researcher to admit or say that a place ever gave them the creeps, but Yorktown Hospital is definitely one of those places for reasons I will explain that definitely will always be in my mind as to the extreme paranormal activity we witnessed and encountered there.

Photo By: Dan LaFave

Yorktown Hospital was opened and run by the Catholic Diocese sometime in the early 50's to serve as a main hospital for all the populations in that rural area. Back in those days in rural areas such as this in Texas, there were not many good medical treatment facilities to go for emergency cases and other things. It was also hard for people to find good doctors in out of the way areas such as these.

The hospital which consists of approximately 30,000 square feet and has a full basement, and two other floors besides a small 3rd top level is shaped like the letter T lying on the ground. Walking around inside this hospital, a person can get lost quite easily, especially at night. The hospital corridors are very spooky and dark, even during the daytime. A person can hear voices during the daytime while walking around. These voices will sound so distinct, that a person will swear that someone is there and playing pranks or something in trying to hide. You can hear many strange noises throughout this hospital and it seems there is always something moving about unseen by the naked eye. It is a very ominous feeling at times and can really put a person on edge. Sometimes it is best just to have someone else there with you so that you do not think you are losing your mind when encountering very strange things.

The old emergency room area is to the right and back of the hospital as well as where the main operating rooms were. The old maternity ward section of the hospital was on the main level and to the far left side wing of the hospital. It is said that many people have heard both child and woman screams very late at night and even throughout the day emanating from that section. The hospital also went through different phases and also once served as a drug rehabilitation center.

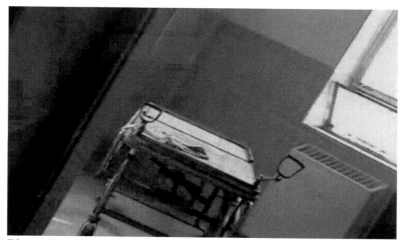

Photo By: Dan LaFave

When walking around in the hospital, a person will notice really quickly that a lot of the old medical equipment was left behind and still within the old hospital which adds to the very strange feeling you get while walking within its dark corridors.

Photo By: Dan LaFave

Even though some people feel comfortable with the dolls in that room, I felt that I just could not be in that room very long and felt very strange. Maybe it was the fact that I felt that I was being watched by the many dolls........I really don't know. This room especially at night in the extreme darkness of Yorktown Hospital really seemed to feel very creepy. During our investigation late that night, there were two instances where we heard pretty loud audible screams that sounded like coming from children. One of those child-like screams was captured very loudly while we were filming where anyone can go to our YouTube channel "Seeking The Paranormal Truth" to watch that video segment and hear the scream. All investigators present at the time heard it very clearly when it occurred. One can easily say that late at night, there were no children present anywhere near that hospital to make that scream. And we all determined that it sounded like it came from within the actual hospital.

The other unique thing again about the hospital is the fact that a lot of the medical equipment was left over as seen here in these two pictures.

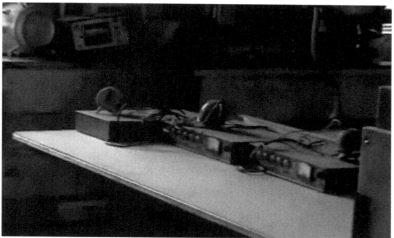

Photo By: Dan LaFave

Photo By: Dan LaFave

We all figured and ascertained that the old medical equipment was all left behind because it was very outdated by the time Yorktown Hospital closed its doors for good in the early 1980's and lay sitting for several years with no use. There was no actual morgue in the hospital, but there is a morgue table where possible examinations took place. Also, in the back lower area of the hospital, there is a really large chapel area. This chapel area is much larger than in other hospitals I have been in, and it is believed this was due to the fact that this hospital again was run by the Catholic Diocese by and order of nuns known as the "Felician Sisters".

Photo By: Dan LaFave

Even though there is a chapel within Yorktown Hospital, I admit that I also felt very strange things within the chapel area. A person would think that you would feel relaxed in there, but many people do not during either tours or paranormal investigations that take place.

As to our team doing the paranormal investigation documentary that night in July 2009, we decided that we would film as much of our investigation as was possible. One of the things we encountered with this was that several of our cameras seemed to lose power much too quickly. For instance, on one of my video cameras, I have a really powerful expensive battery that is supposed to provide 6 hours of battery life. While we did this investigation, it seemed that I was having to charge that camera every hour or so which became much worse as the nightly paranormal investigation wore on.

I found myself constantly having to plug cameras in to re-charge them which made it of course very difficult to try to film things throughout the 8 hour very controlled paranormal investigation that we conducted. One of our purposes as to doing this very controlled investigation was to confirm paranormal activity found by people and also to help show to the world what was actually taking place within this hospital as to paranormal/supernatural means. When you investigate a location such as this, any serious paranormal investigator/researcher wants to share as much good confirmed paranormal activity evidence as they can to the world as to proving the existence of real ghostly occurrences.

About an hour and half into our paranormal investigation that night, things suddenly started to get extreme. This situation is again shown on the paranormal video documentary we did that is shown on YouTube. We had decided to go down to the basement area. In describing the basement area, there is only one way to say it.......you definitely do not want to be by yourself down there during either the day or night. At nighttime, it is of course a lot worse as to the feeling because you are suddenly immersed in complete darkness that envelopes you. When I say this, you can practically poke your eye out with your finger, and never see your finger or hand right in front of your face. As serious paranormal investigators/researchers, we most of the time investigate within very dark conditions late at night. This is not to say that the paranormal/supernatural does not exist as well within very bright daytime hours, but at night it is a lot quieter and more controllable as to any outside sources such as vehicle noise and other things. Late at night, most of the world is asleep and a lot quieter, but we are usually doing our thing investigating sometimes very scary places again in complete darkness with just Infra-Red Camcorders to show our paths of travel within these buildings.

While going down into the Yorktown Hospital basement area with two of my fellow investigators/associates doing the actual investigating, I took it upon myself to just do the actual filming of them and keep totally quiet while doing so. I wanted to make sure that I tracked everything that they did and what they saw, heard, or encountered. This again is very hard at times because we are in complete darkness and the camera-person usually is either in front of them or behind them with only the actual light from the IR viewfinder to show the way. It a lot of times is hard to move about quietly without knocking or banging into things. Also, the camera-person a lot of times you have to remember is experiencing, hearing, and feeling paranormal/supernatural things just like the investigators who are being filmed at the time. Anything and I say anything again can happen to either the investigators or the camera-person at any given time and usually does.

While filming and investigating with the other two paranormal investigators in the basement, we went through a maze of different very dark rooms with equipment looking for things and seeing if things would happen. We all felt we were not alone and being watched and our emotions were high from this, but we never expected what occurred next to happen to us when we were at the far end of the basement coming back out into the main basement hallway area. I at this time was trailing the other two investigators while filming their actions in what they were doing. Every few seconds, I would have to aim the camcorder down so that I could actually see myself and keep from running into things. They both emerged into the main basement hallway area and I was a few steps behind them when I suddenly felt something coming up behind me. It is hard to explain, but I could just feel an ominous presence a few feet away behind me coming towards the doorway. I was at this point coming out into the main hallway area myself, and was about to turn the video camcorder towards that area where I was feeling this, when suddenly something unseen picked up a big wooden two by four that was sitting in that room we just came out of and chunked it straight at us by the doorway. When this occurred, I literally jumped and hit the ceiling. Even seasoned paranormal researchers do this at times when things really shock and surprise us.

All three of us froze at that moment for a second, which is event again on the video that we posted of this investigation event. I then gestured towards the other two investigators and pointed for them to go back inside the other room very quickly as to investigating and determining the source of what just happened which they did. I again am the founder and lead investigator of the team, but I was in the capacity at that time of being the camera-person and did not want the film to show that I was present at the time. I wanted to document and capture the actions of the other two paranormal investigators with me in what they did and said. This is very hard times when extreme paranormal events like what happened occur. It is not every day in a seasoned paranormal researcher's life that a ghostly spiritual hostile entity actually picks up something that large and throws it at investigators in its' fury as to us being there.

After a few minutes, one of the investigators did actually locate the large wooden board that had been picked up and thrown at us. It was lying near the wall that it had banged off of when it was thrown at us. We went through debunking process (process we do as to carefully examining, experimenting, as to ruling out any possible natural explanation) and were able to determine that it indeed was the same wooden board that was thrown at us from the same sound that it made when thrown and hitting that wall. It was determined that something ominous had picked up and thrown that board probably a good 5 to 7 feet with enough loud force to make a really loud noise in almost hitting us. To say the least, that paranormal/supernatural event really got our attention and the night was still very young considering we were only about two and a half hours into our paranormal investigation at that point of time.

We found ourselves upstairs for several minutes talking in disbelief at what had just occurred to us. We also continually watched the camcorder video as to the extreme paranormal event that just unfolded right in front of us. When the event occurred, we had the feeling that we were not wanted in the basement. It was again a very ominous feeling and we had very mixed feelings about going back down to the basement that night to investigate. I can truly say that no one wanted to go back down there.......alone and on their own after that experience.

Earlier that evening, we had officially interviewed the owner Phil Ross, Jo Ann Rivera, Angelka Rogers, and also Mike Hanson, who as well led us on a very good detailed tour of the hospital. They all told us very good information on everything they had experienced while being there at the hospital. Angelka, also a good paranormal friend of ours, had explained that while giving tours of the hospital during the day, that many people including her had very strange paranormal experiences that ranged from hearing and seeing things to physically being manipulated in ways. Jo Ann Rivera described how at times she would get this much disoriented feeling while walking within the hospital, especially down by the Maternity Ward area. Both she and Angelka Rogers told us about the times they saw apparitions and heard the screams and many other things within the hospital both during the day and late at night.

When Mike Hanson, took us around the hospital on a video documented detailed tour, he described both his and his girlfriends many ghostly encounters within the hospital. He would describe at times seeing apparitions of what looked like doctors, nurses, possibly nuns, and patients still walking the hallways. Sometimes he said it appeared these ghostly apparitions were just doing what they would normally be doing without noticing him and other times it appeared the apparitions directly saw and were trying to interact. Angelka Rogers told us of the sometimes many medical mistakes that took places because possibly of the outdated training or inaptitude or age of the doctors who worked there many decades ago. She had described in detail as to some major medical mistakes that appeared to be made by a certain doctor that quite possibly led to the deaths of some person that maybe could have been prevented. It makes a person wonder if sometimes there were mistakes made during possible childbirth that could have led to severe pain or even death to some women or children. One never really knows the truths until further much deeper research is done. What we can say for certain is that medical practices were much different back then as to what they are today as to preventing things. There was also the extreme story told by us by Mike Hanson that once while the hospital was a drug rehabilitation center, that a young man who overdosed on drugs was dropped off by his friends back by the back emergency room entrance late one night and they just left him there possibly because of the drug reasons. No one knows for sure if they rang the back door bell or not. It appears that the nuns quite possibly discovered his lifeless body later that night back by that back emergency room entrance. Many people believe that his name was possibly T.J. and that he is one of the spirits lingering within the hospital.

There is also the story of a violent homicide lover triangle situation that took place down in one of the areas of the hospital basement between 3 people (two males and a female) where an actual shooting took place and possibly one or more of them were killed during the altercation. Anyone looking up at the wall area down there, it does appear that at one time there was actual blood splattered up on the wall possibly from the gunshots and extreme violence that took place that day.

Photo By: Dan LaFave

We were told upon the initial walk-through discussion with Mike Hanson also that sometimes the old equipment could still be heard running like the old ventilators and things back by the old emergency room area even though nothing is plugged in and that there is no electricity as to even being able to run those old machines. He also said that at times you can still strongly smell medicinal things such as antibiotics or antiseptic things in that area even though those were removed long ago. It seems that at many times the hospital does seem to cross over into another dimension as to sight, sound, or smell. Mike also described a story one day when he was alone in the hospital down the main long hallway area at one side and he suddenly saw what looked like a shimmering figure down at the other end of the hallway by one of the old medical machines. He said about that same time he swore that he could hear that machine possibly running or making a noise. When I asked him in more detail as to what the shimmering effect of the figure looked like, he described it very closely to resembling that of the look of the Predator creature in those movies. He said that it appeared to have a metallic looking shimmering effect to it and appeared to be a person. When he walked towards it to get a better look, he said that it just dissipated and disappeared as he tried to get a closer look.

As we setup up our base station earlier that night by the nurses station we started to really think about all the stories and encounters that were explained to us. Many things were told to us, some of them quite extreme. There was another story of a paranormal team that had come in and was also doing a walk-through of the hospital. When they entered the old hospital kitchen area, one of the women said that she felt some pain and burning on her arm. She apparently was wearing a leather jacket at the time that exhibited no signs of damage or tearing where she felt the pain. When she took off her leather jacket to look, it is said that she had red bloody scratches on her arm where she had felt the pain and burning sensation. Another story was out there as well about another paranormal team that had ventured into the basement during their investigation and it appears that a dark black very ominous shadow figure mass came down the hallway towards the group and appeared to envelope one of the male investigators knocking him down in the process, as if in an attack or aggressive mode.

There is believed to be as many as 4 to 5 possible ghostly spirits haunting this hospital on pretty regular basis and other very unique sightings and experiences of other things at times. Now, this does not occur to everyone that visits or investigates at this hospital. You see, the paranormal/supernatural is not something that occurs all the time. It occurs to different people at different times, and that is another thing that really perplexes researchers. No one really at this time has the answers to why this sometimes occurs the way that it does. The reality is that these things are occurring to very rational people who a lot of times have never had a ghostly paranormal experience before. In other words, they are not looking to have an experience......it just happens to them for some unexplainable reason. Yorktown Hospital is a very special place as to the paranormal/supernatural because of how mysterious all of this really is.

When someone goes into that hospital, there is no way of knowing what exactly will occur to them. They may have nothing occur to them, but at the same time they may have the extreme paranormal event of a lifetime occur to them. As to why the ghostly spirits are there in the hospital, this was another big question that we as paranormal researchers have. Perhaps it is because of wrongful things or quite possibly untimely deaths that occurred within the hospital......maybe it is something a lot more perplexing than just that. Maybe dimensions of time are crossing over at times, and these instances are showing visions and sounds from another time. These are all quite reasonable thoughts for any serious paranormal investigator/researcher to have. When a person ventures and walks the hallways and rooms of old Yorktown Hospital in looking at a lot of the old equipment that still exists within the building, it really makes a rational person wonder as to these many solid and viable questions.

Photo By: Dan LaFave

Our paranormal investigation team, Graveyard Shift Paranormal, again had many strange eventful things occur to us during that long nightly investigation. While sitting at the base station that we set up by the nurse's station, I could not help but keep looking over to the old phone on the wall that the nurse's used to call outside and to all the patient rooms. There was another event that another paranormal team had once when they were sitting in this same exact spot one night, when they claim that phone rang very loudly several times. When they got up to look and answer the phone, they again realized something about that phone and the rest of the hospital. There all the original electrical and phone lines did not work and had not worked for many years. The story says that they picked up the phone, only to hear nothing.....even though it had run seconds before.

All these thoughts and what we had encountered that night up to that point were all going through my head as I again sat at the base station taking a break. It was very hot in the hospital that July night, most likely in the 90's where a lot of times we were all dripping in sweat with our t-shirts soaked. There were also other times when chilled air seemed to come down the hallways and within an instant I felt very cooled off again with all my sweat perspiration literally disappearing within seconds only to have that same cool sensation leave minutes later and the very hot temperature come back. What exactly that was, no one really knows. Serious paranormal investigators/researchers like us encounter these types of things sometimes on regular basis in the environments that we investigate......they can consist of either extreme cold or hot spots that emanate out of no where.

As I again was sitting there, was thinking about all of this and of the previous situation where the wooden board had been picked up and thrown at us, the screams we heard at times, the strange sensations we were all feeling, the constant feeling of being watched, the strange knocking response noises we got on our questions, and the sometime movement noises we heard down the hallway from us.....even though no one was there. I was looking at our video cameras which again appeared to be drained unnaturally by something, considering the batteries on these cameras should have lasted for hours but seemed to only be providing minutes at a time before having to plug them in and recharge them again.

We had one lone power source cable coming in through the back of the hospital off the pole there, by which we got our power. Because again, this hospital has not regular electricity running through its old power lines and cables. I looked at my wife Connie approximately 3 am and told her that we needed to go down to the basement and run a very good EVP (Electronic Voice Phenomenon) recording session to see what else we could discover or find. In looking at our video cameras one last time, I determined that we would have to leave them behind......because it was taking a lot of time to recharge them. We decided to go down into the basement, just the two of us, without any flashlights and just our two digital audio recorders. Again, this hospital is very dark in that you literally cannot see your hand in front of your face without a light source.

When I and my wife Connie walked down the stairs towards the basement area, we both could feel something even though we weren't saying anything. We stopped a few times while walking because I could swear that something or someone was walking behind us. It again was just the two of us, the rest of our team stayed upstairs by the base station area. First, we were talking about going back to the same area in the basement where the board had been picked up and thrown at us earlier that night, but we both decided instead to go to the other side area of the basement......the same area where the past reported shooting murder event had occurred. Hardly anyone ever goes back into that area at night to investigate. We walked slowly because we again both had a very difficult time trying to see in front of us as to where we were going.

This old hospital is rather large for it's time and area at around 30,000 square feet. Sure, there are much larger hospitals out there, but the way Yorktown Hospital is designed and laid out is different which gives you the feeling that it is much larger. There are many winding corridors where a person can easily get turned around or lost in at night if you do not have a flashlight. We again had no flashlight with us, and it was planned this way. We stumbled along towards that area going through a few heavy steel doors. We then found a spot to stand in that very dark area. With what happened to us next, we both wished we had taken a flashlight and video camcorder with us.

We both started our digital audio recorders and were standing next to each other approximately 3 feet apart. I was standing to the left of my wife. At first, it did not feel strange, but then the environment seemed to change. I could feel something strange but could not put my finger on it. I am sure my wife Connie was feeling the same thing even though we weren't making any comments about that. Connie started to ask questions the same way that we always do during the controlled EVP recording sessions that we do. She started off by asking if there was anyone there and what their name or names were. During these EVP recording sessions, we would always tag any noises that we knew were natural (such as stomach growling, vehicle going by outside on road, dog barking, and any noise we knew was not paranormal). This was so that when we went back later to listen to our recordings, we could easily identity those natural occurring noises versus what may be considered paranormal. We also as a rule never whisper, even though sometimes that does happen, where again we tag any whispers. We talk out loud just like we are talking to another person, which in ghostly reality world we really are quite possibly talking to someone who used to be living in the existence we are accustomed to.

We would always do a customary EVP session of guidelines where we pause 10 seconds after each question that is asked out loud. We would also have pretty much a set of standard questions we always ask, but also questions that have to do with the place/location or people/names who used to be associated if those names are known to us. A lot of times we do have a lot of information to use before the investigation, because we have already done our homework as to gathering known information through research and talking with people. With history, this is very important especially when we are researching any historical sites with known historical figures. While Connie asked the first set of questions, I suddenly could feel the hair on the back of my neck and arms stand up again. It was pretty much the same feeling I had previously that night right before the wooden board was picked up and thrown at us. If I remember, I do believe Connie also asked at that time if it was them who had done that to us in the basement. Even though I could not see anything due to the darkness, I started to turn my head and look around the room. There was a water drip from a pipe down there in the basement as well which to me seemed to make the situation a bit more nervous. At that moment, I could not again put my finger on it, but I felt that something was going to happen to us. But, of course, I had no idea what at that point.

Connie continued to ask questions, and I started to ask some questions as well. It was then that we both started to hear movement noises in that basement area with us. The scary thing again is that we both were just standing there and not moving. The complete blackness around us made it even worse at that moment because the feeling you have at that moment as a seasoned investigator is that we came to find the paranormal.........and here it is now. It is a feeling and mix of adrenaline and I must admit a degree of fear and uncertainty woven in. Only someone who has done this and who has really experienced this knows that exact feeling. Connie asked me at that time out loud if I was creating the footsteps. I told her no, that I was still standing in the same spot approximately 3 to 4 feet from her.

We again could see nothing around us due to the extreme blackness which strangely at that time seemed to really be oppressing itself upon us. It was at that moment that I heard a very loud male whisper voice to the right of me and Connie. At that very same moment, Connie yelled out for me to quit messing with her and asked where I was in the room in relation to her. I yelled out, "Hon, I heard that also and that was not me, I am standing over here". We were both very alarmed then by what just happened and I could hear that Connie was starting to get a little distressed by the sound of her voice. I emphasized to her that we need to stay still and not move and keep going. Which you see, would have been very hard for most paranormal minded investigators/researchers at that moment, even the seasoned ones.......because the real feeling and emotion we had that moment was ominous and for us to get out of there. Most people would have bolted due to what was happening to us and not being able to see anything due to the extreme darkness.

We continued to ask questions at that point and both were looking nervously around the room. I know I was, am pretty sure my wife was doing the same. We were nervous but very fascinated at the same time with what was occurring at that moment. That moment we are all looking for with the paranormal/supernatural.......that moment of when intelligent contact occurs. It was then that we heard another movement in front of us about 10 to 15 feet and then with a very loud force we heard something slam against the far concrete wall that echoed throughout the whole basement room section we were in. Now those just about made us want to get out of there. My wife Connie screamed out again thinking that I had done it. I told her again that no, that was not me, that something or someone had just picked up something and thrown it. I started to walk over to that area to try to see. Connie said no, don't go over there, I want to ask more questions to see if it will answer. It was at that moment that we heard more footsteps around us and what sounded like another voice possibly answering her. I had to go over there and did and discovered upon bending down that I felt a plastic bottle on the floor. A bottle that looked like it had been crushed from the force of being thrown and slammed against the concrete wall really hard. I walked back over to Connie and showed her. We were just amazed by what we were seeing and experiencing but again we both felt that something was not good with this......that it appeared to be ominous or very aggressive towards us.

It was at these moments that I wished that I had the video camcorders with us to try to record what was occurring besides what was being picked up on our digital audio recorders. I started to go and get a camera, but then thought no......with our luck, by the time I get back it will be gone, and did not want to leave my wife alone in that room. We continued with our questions and then heard something actually walk a complete circle around us within a distance of say 10 feet, we could hear it moving in front of us, to the side of us, to the back of us, and then in front of us again. When you hear things like this, you simply know that it is not an animal or naturally occurring from something.......this sounded just like a two legged person walking around us. The question we both had at the time was what else it is going to do to us as to interacting. I admit that I was shaking while this experience was taking place, am sure Connie was also. It is just a natural human reaction to when extreme paranormal/supernatural activity occurs. You think you are totally ready for it as to what might happen, but in reality, a person never really is and is very much surprised and shocked to experience these very unnatural unexplainable things.

After approximately 20 to 25 minutes of constant things such as movement, footsteps, and some audible voices occurring, as suddenly as it started.....it stopped. Both myself and my wife Connie then decided to head back up and could not wait to tell the other investigators up at the base station as to what we had just encountered. Upon heading out of that room and entering the basement hallway area next to where the stairs were, we both stopped suddenly. It was at that moment that we could hear 2 to 3 footsteps right behind us that also stopped then. We had our recorders still going at that time. We felt that it was indeed following us. I took one of the camcorders and gave it to one of the other investigators and told him and Connie that we needed to head back down to that basement with the camcorder to see if it would happen again and we could document on camera this time besides just the digital audio recorders. We then headed back down the stairs to the basement.

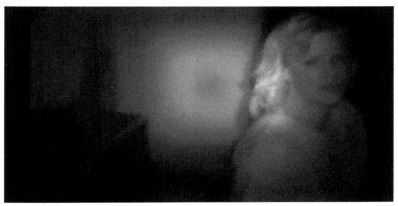

Photo By: Dan LaFave

Photo By: Dan LaFave

Upon going back down to the basement area, we did another EVP recording session for approximately 15 minutes this time with the video camcorder going. We could feel however that the environment was not the same, that there was no longer that strange very ominous feeling within that basement room area. It was frustrating to us considering what had just occurred to us and now here we were with a video camcorder recording and nothing was happening. Could it be that it now knew we had a camera and that we no longer were shroud in complete darkness where it could play with our minds in doing things to us? It certainly felt that it knew what it was doing and that it was intelligent and aggressive.

Nothing else strange occurred that night as we packed all the equipment and attempted to sleep the few hours towards morning till the sun came up and we headed back home 4 hours on the highway. We could not wait to review and analyze all our possible paranormal evidence and we found that we had captured very amazing clear and loud Class A ghostly Eva's during the course of the investigation. While on break getting water, my wife Connie had laid down her digital audio recorder with it still recording our conversation when a loud echoing ominous ghostly voice can be heard saying clearly the word "Holy" possibly in reference to fact that this hospital was once run by the Roman Catholic

40

system. There were also EVP's from the basement when I and my wife Connie were down there during the extreme time and an aggressive ghostly male EVP voice can be heard saying "Stupid Bitch" to her questions and that one loud male whisper can be heard trying to get our attention.

There were many extreme very unique ghostly paranormal/supernatural memories and experiences that our team Graveyard Shift Paranormal Investigations had that night in July 2009 that we will never forget. Yorktown Hospital to us is a very special place for real ghostly research to be done in trying to find out the answers to the many questions that we have about the paranormal. The television show "Ghost Adventures" even went there in February 2011 to film a very interesting documented television episode in which many things were also discovered by them. We plan on going back to Yorktown Hospital for a return trip and a very special documented paranormal investigation to try to find out a whole lot more. If you want to truly experience ghostly haunted activity on a personal level, I highly recommend that you pay a visit to Yorktown Hospital to see for yourself........if you can handle it.

Chapter 3: Helena, Texas

Photo By: Dan LaFave

    I was contacted several years ago while we were lead paranormal researchers on another serious paranormal Texas based team by a resident of this now almost gone forgotten ghost town. A resident whose house was in very close proximity to the old large historic Karnes County courthouse and museum that sat there. This house sat only about a hundred feet or so from this old historic courthouse and other historic buildings of the ghost town Helena. A person standing there could imagine the old ghost town on both sides of the now modern looking highway. Someone living there in modern times could have a hard time to imagining what that exact area might have looked 200 years ago. It would have been much different in those days of the old west. When we had investigated this house years ago, we really had no idea at that point just how much the ghostly paranormal world was going to interact with people.

Photo By: Dan LaFave

Back then in those days, we found very real confirmed ghostly paranormal activity within her home but were never quite sure why that was there. They even personally once picked up a recording of a voice saying that there was hidden gold buried somewhere on their property by a tree, but a search never uncovered anything. Perhaps there is gold buried in many spots around Helena. It is believed that the KGC (Knights of the Golden Circle) possibly hid and buried gold all over the South and possibly in Helena. They would bury gold coins a lot of times in Mason jars buried at the base of marked trees by which they put their symbols on. They did this because a lot of gold during the Civil War was supposedly hid by the South as to helping the South finance the war. There were also some famous outlaws associated and said to be a member of the KGC.....most notably Jesse James.

Some of the paranormal activity found and encountered by us and them in her house and in that area seemed ominous at times, but again we did not know for certain why. We concluded that paranormal investigation at the time with the thinking that the sometimes strong paranormal activity was there, but again........we did not know exactly why or how.

Now, here we were again, both myself, my wife Connie, and our own very serious paranormal team years later to see what else we could possibly find as to why this paranormal activity was taking place at times and to explore more about the history of this old historic Texas ghost town and how that all might possibly tie into the sometimes extreme ghostly activity occurring to people at various times.

We unpacked all of our various field paranormal investigation equipment that consisted of different digital audio recorders (with names like Sony, Olympus, and RCA), different EMF (Electro-Magnetic Field Meters) like the Mel-Meter, Tri-Field Natural, The Ghost Meter (both initial and Pro model), our 8 channel DVR system with several what we call static infrared and full-spectrum cams, Experimentation Ovilus X, PSB-7 ITC Experimentation Spirit Box, FLIR camera, full-spectrum digital cameras, full-spectrum and Infra-Red individual camcorders, ambient temperature meters, EFP EVP Field Processor, laser grid pattern lights, walkie-talkies, and various other paranormal equipment that we used during these very controlled paranormal investigations.

Photo By: Dan LaFave

We soon met up with our good friend Barry Harrin, who is the author of "Helena, Texas – The Toughest Town On Earth" available for sale on Amazon and off his website, and discussed particulars of what we were going to do and how exactly we were going to investigate that night. We also discussed a lot of things more personally about Helena, Texas history with him and it's brutal past. In his very good book, Barry explains how a lot of us have watched great western movies with stars like Gary Cooper, John Wayne, and Clint Eastwood, but that no western movie stands out from the rest like "Gunfight at the O.K. Corral" in which a famous documented shootout took place in Tombstone, Arizona between good and evil in a sense. Barry also went on to describe to us that if we really believed that Tombstone in those days was a tough place, that we were in for a shocking reality check as to the hidden story of Helena, Texas and that area of Texas kept from history books which made the shooting event at Tombstone look like a Sunday picnic.

Barry Harrin went on to explain to us that much of old Texas and the South history has been omitted and kept out of history books as to how it actually occurred. He does not know why but through many years of personal research he has found many omitted important history facts about Texas and Helena, Texas and that area that appear to have been purposely kept out of the history books. Could this be that some historians did not really want people to know how hostile and brutal a place this really was in those days? Could it be that there were internal politics at play quite possibly that leads to why a lot of important history is portrayed to us one way versus another as to how actual history events unfolded. The truth is that no one knows for sure because many things change over time when it comes to history and how it is told, but there again were many intriguing things that Barry told us as to what actually took place in Helena, Texas back in the 1800's when it was a thriving developing area with a large population for the time before demise and a possible curse were afflicted upon this old community leading to it eventually turning into a Texas ghost town.

This is how the brutal story goes as to why Barry and we believe for the reasons that the present-day ghost town of Helena, Texas may possibly be haunted with ghostly paranormal activity the way that it is. It was a dark and very cold day back on December 26, 1884 with a lot of freezing snow and sleet that most likely kept a lot of people indoors. A person can imagine an old town with many wooden buildings lining the street very much like western movies portray them except that they did not look glamorous in the way some movies depict these old western towns to be. Being so close and after Christmas, locals were most likely still tired and inside from all the festivities associated with the holiday.

Western days in those times consisted of a lot of drinking of whiskey and other liquor and it is said that Helena had many saloons in those days lining the whole main mud road/highway that was the center of town. It is said that due to how this town was growing in those days as to population and money, that there were 13 saloons. Now some people consider the number 13 unlucky......what do you think? Sheriff Edgar Leary was doing his best in trying to keep the law and order within this bustling town which also appeared to have a lot of control and corruption taking place by people of wealth and power who lived in the area, mainly William Green Butler who was the richest rancher in old Karnes County at the time. As Barry told us all of this very intriguing information and other things he had uncovered, I could not help but personally think that a lot of western movies show this very thing taking place as to some power baron of wealth doing everything they could to control an area and its' people by their own political means. This most likely took place a lot more in those days than most people know.

Barry Harrin went on to tell us that there was bad blood between Sheriff Edgar Leary and William Green Butler due to the fact that while Butler had been out driving his cattle up the historic Chisholm Trail to Kansas, that the sheriff had busted into Butler's mansion on his land as to his attempt in trying to find Butler's 20 year old son Emmett who was wanted for questioning as to possibly murdering an African-American man somewhere in Wilson County. But Emmett was not to be found there. It appears that the senior Butler was furious once this information was found out.

Once Emmett Butler and his sidekick Hugh McDonald found out down the road in the next town, it appears that they drunkenly started on their way back to avenge this situation of the Butler home invasion by the sheriff and his deputies. The next stormy day, it is said that the townspeople and sheriff knew that Emmett Butler was coming. It appears that everyone was waiting to see what would happen. As Emmett and his sidekick road into town, the sheriff and his deputies quickly cornered them and demanded that they surrender their guns. The other rider did so quickly, but Emmett Butler did not.

Emmett Butler turned and drew his six gun revolver and a single shot rang out......with the bullet hitting the sheriff in the chest and killing him. As he was falling, the sheriff yelled out in extreme pain from the pain in his chest that he was shot, and Emmett got back on his horse and started to ride out of town......only to be gunned down with many shots fired at him from the different buildings to die later that evening. The thing is that several shots were fired at him from many buildings by many people, and appeared that the town had taken up arms in dealing with the situation. When the elder William Butler found out of this situation involving the death of his son, he rode back to Helena to claim the body of his son and find out who did it. When he got to Helena with his gang of cowboys, they could not find a single soul as the residents of Helena all hid.

It is said that he yelled, "I want to know who killed my son!" Still no answer or sight from anyone as he yelled this again many times up and down the main dirt road there in Helena. He then it is believed to have taken his personal vengeance out and cursed the town of Helena when he yelled next "This town killed my son; now I am going to kill this town!!" The town was due possibly to have the railroad either come through or very close to Helena in those days. It is believed that William Green Butler did indeed live by his word, wrath, and power by making sure that the railroad instead went many miles past Helena and essentially living out the curse as to Helena dying and becoming the ghost town it is today. It is also believed by some that quite possibly their ghosts and other ghosts of Helena still linger due to this event and the curse by Butler.

Our paranormal team that night for our investigation was going to split off as to investigating different locations around the old historic Helena, Texas ghost town. When we split off, we usually split into 3 member groups (two actual people investigating while one person films them investigating). This is because we want to create good real filming perspectives of our paranormal investigations to share with the public as to exactly what we encounter, witness, or discover as to sometimes scary ghostly paranormal/supernatural activity. To give any viewers of our paranormal investigation videos on YouTube and our website a good feel of what the real paranormal/supernatural world was like in various interesting historical locations.

We heard from Barry Harrin, his two sons, and his ex-wife Lydia, and others that over the past several months, there had been many very strange unnatural things happening to people at times in there and other buildings around the ghost town. This involved hearing strange voices and noises, being touched, and very strange EVP (Electronic Voice Phenomenon) recordings of women crying as if being tortured, dragging and footstep sounds, and what sounded like a brutal violent man with an old creepy Texas southern accent saying to "Get Out" as if they were invading his domain. All of this obtained while they were exploring personally for themselves to see what they might encounter.

We found all of this information very fascinating and intriguing, but were very unsure for ourselves on what we were to encounter personally deep into the night during this very controlled in-depth paranormal investigation within several historic buildings of the old Texas ghost town.

It was approximately 8 pm; the same time that I, my wife Connie, and our paranormal team/group Graveyard Shift Paranormal Investigations usually started our many controlled detailed investigations. There was no moon that night. We had traveled nearly 4 hours this day on the highway to this mysterious historic forgotten Texas ghost town called Helena, Texas. This was a place that someone could drive past quite easily without even noticing because of how it has shrunk over time. Once we gathered and distributed our paranormal equipment, both myself, my wife Connie, and one of our fellow paranormal researchers/associates Harvey Martinez headed over to investigate one of the old buildings with reported high paranormal activity within from several very reliable and credible sources.

This old building was at one time the Masonic Lodge (where it is believed the KGC – Knights of the Golden Circle, a notorious group, also used to hang out in the 1800's). In front of the Masonic Lodge to the right as can be seen in this picture here is one of the surviving old hangman trees where it is believed several people were hung by the rope till dead in the 1800's, many of them believed to be innocent of what they were accused of. It is believed by some that Helena might have been one of the KGC's main secret meeting areas as to planning out things for The Civil War. There is a possibility that this might be true because there are still many unsolved mysteries from long ago where the facts and truth are not readily known. The KGC operation was very secret in how they did things. It is still believed that much of that information and history is still hidden waiting to be discovered.

Photo By: Dan LaFave (Hangman's Tree To Right)

The old dated Masonic order/charter is still posted on the wall to view. As we entered and started our paranormal investigation around 9 pm that night within the Masonic Lodge, we all started to feel extreme things around us in which we knew we were not alone. We were standing there in the extreme darkness trying to get our eyes to adjust looking at things when suddenly the environment around us began to change. We could feel it. We knew that we were no longer alone and that we were indeed within someone else's domain, possibly that we stepped into another time in history. We could feel the hair on our arms, necks, and heads suddenly stand up. There suddenly was an extreme feeling of electricity and energy in the dark large room around us. That feeling we experienced sometimes in certain paranormal environments when something very unnatural and wild was about to occur. We all felt that soulful feeling where even though there were three of us in that room, we all suddenly felt alone.

In that total darkness while all three of us were standing very still with the front door entirely closed, we suddenly very loudly and clearly could hear movement and footsteps coming towards us from the back area. The personal feeling was as if something unseen was stalking and watching us.

Was it an animal? No, it quite clearly was not. We all looked towards that area. Suddenly, we got the answer we were looking for when a large rock picked up off the floor by something was thrown very hard against the deteriorating wood ceiling structure right above our heads to then land and bounce at our feet. In a second, we all looked up first trying to focus our eyes to the rattling vibrating ceiling structure above and then to the large cement rock laying now at our feet. We all could feel and sense it then with an alarming sense.......the unseen.....when one of us gasped loudly "Oh God!"

We all turned our heads trying focus into the darkness with the lenses of our infrared camcorders at that moment, but it seemed as if the darkness was trying to swallow us up. It is those moments when you feel and hear something extreme as to the paranormal that gets us. It does not matter how long we have been investigating the paranormal up to that point, because it is that scary situation that faces us at that moment where we wonder what will happen next. Will it go away or will something violent occur to us? We also wonder what exactly is there in the darkness watching and moving around us. Also, what does it want to do to us?

These are all questions that go through investigators heads at moments such as this, and this was the feeling we all had at the time. We stared into that darkness towards the back of the old Masonic Lodge and yelled, "Who's there, make yourself known!" Now, this sounds silly when you hear it, but at those moments, an investigator does not really know what to say from the actual shock of the situation. It sounds funny because we have already heard or possibly seen something ominous there, and now we are calling it to come out and possibly do something to us. A paranormal investigator knows that anything and say it again 'anything' can happen during paranormal investigations. Sometimes nothing happens at all, but when the scary paranormal stuff occurs, it is usually pretty extreme. As we stared into that darkness, we were again all feeling that anticipation of something extreme to occur.

As we stood there, we could hear something moving beyond that veil of darkness that it seemed even our infrared camcorders could not see. It seemed to be moving beyond the focus of both our eyes and the camcorders infrared lights. The question we had then was is this thing intelligent? And what exactly are we dealing with here? We could easily tell that the movement noise that which we all heard was not an animal, this noise strongly appeared to be walking on two legs as it shuffled around quickly. A lot of times the walking/movement noises we hear will be in one location of the building at one moment, and within a few moments be entirely in a different location or even behind us. The scary thing is that we will not hear the actual movement noises in the middle, just the walking noises all of a sudden to the front, left, right, or behind us. After several minutes of gasping things under our breath in shock and trying to chase this ghostly unseen force or entity (we use these general terms because we do not really know what they are), we decided to wrap up our investigation session within the Masonic Lodge and move on towards investigating the other old Texas ghost town buildings.

We again were in split groups of two to three investigators as we went to the other locations. The Helena, Texas ghost town now only consists of a few old historic buildings from what it actually was in the 1800's. There is a main highway that goes right through the middle where a lot of trucks travel through now. This modern highway used to be the actual historical dirt highway at one time that went all the way to the much used Indianola port on the Gulf of Mexico where a lot of Civil War supplies were brought in and up to the southern troops up at the battle fronts. Looking at everything now in modern times, it is hard to imagine that Helena, Texas was at one time such a thriving and brutal violent town.

We actually had earlier set up our full 8 static still camera DVR video surveillance system up in the historic Ruckman House which was built in 1878 and which is one of the oldest historical homes in Karnes County within Texas. Built for John Ruckman and his family then, this historic home is very unique because it was built entirely of Cypress tree wood shipped in from Florida.

Photo By: Dan LaFave

This is why this house is still very well preserved and standing versus other woods which would disintegrate and rot over time. We found this old home to be very interesting and big for it's time. The Ruckman House is actually 3 stories tall with an adjoining back area of the house which includes the formal dining/kitchen area as well as the children's bedrooms upstairs. This old home has many rooms as well as a full walk-in attic area which is very creepy at nighttime. Upon standing at the bottom of these stairs at night alone in the house, a person gets a very strange feeling of tension and apprehension. A person while alone in this house at night can simply feel the energy around them. It can sometimes feel quite disturbing as to that feeling. It is a long walk up those dark attic stairs when you are alone. The only way to describe it is that you personally have to be there to feel and experience that feeling. A person definitely feels that they are not alone. As to exactly what or who is there in the house at times, that is a question that still remains to be explored more.

Photo By: Dan LaFave

For some unknown reason, it has been found by our paranormal group and other paranormal people that the Ruckman House has paranormal activity within it. Sometimes this paranormal activity has been extreme for us and for other people. It has also been very interesting as to what we have found. This activity within has included hearing scary audible loud voices calling at us and sometimes by our names. It also has included these same voices calling out to us from somewhere within the house while we are alone in it. We over time, have conducted different paranormal investigations within the Ruckman House and each time we have also gotten very different results, but one fact is clear.......that this house does appear to be haunted due to the sometimes extreme paranormal activity within it.

Again, one of things that I find fascinating is that the paranormal and history at times do seem to mix and this appears to be happening within the historic Ruckman House at times. Why exactly this is occurring, no one really knows, but we do have our possible theories. One of these theories is of a possible time continuum paradox talking place. There is the possibility that we in modern times are possibly crossing over into past times or the opposite taking place. We say this because we really do not know what ghosts really are.

They are perhaps spiritual soul entities (used to be living) as many of us believe or maybe they are a whole more than even that. Maybe they are actual real people seeing, hearing, and experiencing things crossing over that timeline at that exact same time in space that we in our world are? Am sure this sounds really strange, but if you have experienced things the way that we as people who have researched and witnessed this mysterious world for many years now, then you would see and be open to the possibilities here. Within Helena, there have been many very strange encounters that sometimes may be this exact thing taking place. The other possibility is that these spiritual ghostly entities are somehow trapped within these environments for unknown reasons, and are possibly reaching out in innocent but also hostile violent ways sometimes.

I say this because once I was conducting a paranormal investigation within the Ruckman House totally alone up in the attic. Everyone else (approximately 4 to 5 people) were outside well away from the house. We were conducting paranormal experiments to see what would happen when each of us was alone in the house all by ourselves. Not many paranormal investigators will do this kind of thing because of fear of what could occur. When investigators are alone, there is always the possibility of extreme things occurring in locations where frequent strong paranormal activity has previously been confirmed and documented by researchers. The Ruckman House and the ghost town of Helena, Texas are such a historic location that fits this particular situation. We had the 8 channel DVR video surveillance system set up with static cameras all throughout the house and we each took our moment to go inside and investigate for ourselves doing different paranormal experiments. We also filmed ourselves independently as we each went inside this house. We also all took a different part of the big house each time one of us went inside. When it was my turn, I had the very dark and eerie attic area.

As I grabbed my paranormal investigation gear which consisted of 3 digital audio recorders, full-spectrum camcorder, ITC P-SB7 Spirit Box, EFP EVP Field Processor, K2 and other EMF meters, I went slowly in the pitch black darkness slowly floor by floor by myself until I got up to the attic loft area. I could hear my lone footsteps at the time which sounded very hollow as I walked. I found myself stopping several times and listening along the way because I could swear I heard someone else following me. As I proceeded throughout the house, I placed a digital audio recorder recording in a room on the 2nd floor and took the other two recorders with me to use up in the attic area. Once I got up there and set up, I could not hear anything throughout the whole house or outside, and that was a very eerie and creepy feeling to me at the time. It was also very dark in that house that night. I could easily see how someone's imagination could run wild at times such as this, but I stayed very calm and rational as I prepared to do some EVP recording sessions while filming with the full-spectrum camcorder that I had to what I might see or capture as to evidence. I opened up the other attic door there on the loft to open up the other attic area which was even creepier to me than the actual loft area where I was standing carefully observing and listening.

It was a little breezy outside and there were times that the wind would come up and rattle the attic windows a little bit. Whenever that occurred a few times, it took me a little while to figure out that was naturally occurring. There were also natural creeks from within the old cypress wood house that I could hear. Old historic houses a few hundred years old do that at times. After I managed to rationalize these natural things occurring within the house, it was then that I felt a change. This was that same kind of environment change that sometimes occurred with paranormal investigations we sometimes do in unique historic places.

Photo By: Dan LaFave

I could suddenly hear movement off to my right side near the attic stairs. I walked over with the full-spectrum camera and shot it around that area and also down the stairs. As I did this, my camcorder suddenly powered out and shut it off for a moment. What was strange is that this particular camcorder would never do something like this and was actually very hard to turn off, having to actually close the viewfinder on it in doing so. I did this and then opened up the video viewfinder again, and to my amazement the camera started recording again just fine. It also still showed that I had 98% battery power left in it which was almost fully charged. When fully charged, the lithium battery in this camera would give me between 2 to 3 hours video recording time. I would always monitor and make sure as to the battery power and plug in and recharge at certain points of any paranormal investigation.

As I was standing there looking at the camcorder and trying to figure out what had occurred with it, there suddenly again was a movement noise down on the 2nd floor below me that sounded like a person moving about. I went down for a moment and checked the whole 2nd floor with no one or thing there. I then walked back up to the attic and resumed my EVP recording session where I was asking several questions. About 4 to 5 minutes into this, I suddenly heard a very loud movement over by the open attic door by the stairs again. This actually made me jump it was so loud. As I aimed the video camera in that direction and also tried to focus my eyes to the darkness, I then saw something move by the top of the stairs which was a distance of about 15 feet from me. I saw it moved very quickly as well. It had no shape, and really just looked like a quick darting black mass. I was not sure if it went back down the stairs or into the other part of the attic.

As I saw it, I did not really know what to do at that shocking moment and just exclaimed out very loudly, "I think I see you, is that you?" It was at moment that I really jumped when a loud very clear woman's voice came up from the second floor saying "Yes" quite clearly. I got up and moved for the top of the stairs very quickly trying to focus the camcorder the best that I could in being able to see. It was so dark up there, that my natural eyesight was not good; I was dependent on the full-spectrum camcorder viewfinder in seeing everything. As I got to the top of the stairs, and looked down, something scary happened. The camcorder suddenly turned itself off again putting me in complete darkness standing at the top of those stairs. The feeling of being alone really overcame me at that moment because I could not see a thing around me and my flashlight was on the floor fifteen feet away from me on the floor. I started to walk over to where it was and closed and opened the camcorder again and it powered up again normally with the same battery usage life showing on it. At this point, I was starting to feel very disturbed and frustrated. I then heard another noise towards that open attic door and stairs, and turned the camcorder towards it when the camcorder went out again. This occurred several times in the span of 5 minutes of me standing there doing the same thing over and over again till the camcorder finally powered off for good and would not come back on for me.

I found myself constantly looking back over to that area at the top of the stairs by that open attic door wondering what else shocking was going to occur to me. I decided to end my investigation session at that time and go back downstairs with the equipment and try to figure out what was going on with that camcorder. When I got down to the DVR base station surveillance system on the 1st floor, I started to feel more relieved due to the video screen light that was down there. I then started to head out the door, and tried the camcorder again going out.......and found the camcorder came on just fine with plenty of battery power showing. Walking out towards the group of investigators standing outside by the road, I started to tell them what amazing things I had just encountered. As I started to tell them, they all looked at me and asked if I was downstairs at any time messing with the DVR surveillance video system. I told them no, that I was up in the attic the whole time except for the brief moments on the 2nd floor doing things. I never once touched the recording DVR surveillance system down there.

They proceeded to tell me that approximately 5 to 10 minutes of me going up to the attic, they said that the system flickered a few times and then went out completely for a few minutes causing darkness through the door side pane windows before coming back on. They did not want to come inside because they thought it was me doing this. As I determined the time they saw this, I suddenly realized this was the moment that I experienced the video camcorder turning off those 6 to 7 times before powering off totally. As I told them about the very clear loud woman's audible voice coming up in response to my question and then my video camera doing what it did, I suddenly got the chills thinking about the whole situation. Everyone just stood there looking back at me in amazement.

Some who have explored and investigated the Ruckman House have said that they did not get anything or experience anything while others have gone inside at night or daytime and had extreme things occur to them. Our group of course has had the extreme things occur. I have also seen people walk inside and tell us that they feel strange things, but did not know exactly what those things were. Speaking with Barry Harrin, his sons Brian and Brandon, and Barry's ex-wife Lydia, they have experienced a lot of very strange things in that house from hearing things to actually seeing things. They say that at times during the evening while locking up the Ruckman House from historical tours during the day, they will sometimes turn around and see what looks like people (child and a man) looking back at them from inside the house even though there is no one there and house was checked. It is believed by some that the aggressive hostile spirit of a man (possibly a past butcher of pigs) and different spirits of a woman (possibly a slave), boy, and girl are at times there trying to interact with the living. Why they are there no one has the exact answer for. Perhaps they are here because of the long ago curse left upon Helena. The Ruckman House to me and our paranormal group is a fascinating historical place of both beauty and the supernatural.

People including our paranormal group have also encountered things within the old courthouse.

Photo By: Dan LaFave

Once while sitting alone inside the upstairs courtroom area, my wife Connie had her hair touched and stroked. She described the feeling as if by an invisible hand. As she sat there and felt this, she said that it made her jump and turn around. There have also been times when were in there and heard footsteps and strange voices. We have also gotten very clear loud EVP's of people responding to our questions.

These recordings sound like a woman who is possibly looking for help or trying to get our attention towards something she needs. We have also gotten EVP's of a man and children noises/voices when no children were present. It makes a person wonder what things went on in this old courtroom from the past as to people possibly found guilty of crimes that they did not commit......only to be hung later by either of the two hangman trees outside. Only one of these hangman's trees exists now right in front of the Old Masonic Lodge.

Barry had told us also of an encounter/story by another paranormal team while investigating the old farm house that sits closely to the old courthouse. While investigating in one of the bedrooms, this male investigator was apparently in the room staring at an angle into the old antique dresser mirror one night, when he claims to have witnessed the apparition image in the mirror of a woman wearing an older frontier type looking dress walking through the bedroom doorway suddenly holding a candle and looking at him with a look of shock as if she was just as surprised to see him as he was to see her. He then says that the expression on the woman ghostly apparition's face went from a look of shock to a look of confrontation. Then the apparition disappeared as quickly as she appeared.

Barry told me that the investigator was very surprised by what they had just witnessed in that house. While also investigating this strange farmhouse on another occasion, another paranormal team also captured on video to be what looked like a very strange light anomaly above and next to the attic stairs door moving about. I myself looked at this video and found it to be very strange looking. Hardly anyone ever goes up to the attic area of this farmhouse, and our team did not even really know this house had a walk-in attic till we were outside and I noticed an upper window and wondered where that mysterious window went. While investigating this farmhouse, we have obtained very strong EMF spike readings in the kitchen area even though there was no electrical source anywhere close by. The spikes seem to be the highest by the very back door of this kitchen and do come and go. Very strong cold spot areas can also be felt throughout this house that manifest and then dissipate as quickly as they are felt. During different sessions, our team has picked up clear EVP recordings of an old man who appears to say that he is lost and thinks the house is his. He appears confused sounding on the EVP recording. We also have picked up recordings of a woman and children in the house.

The other building we have picked up good paranormal evidence is the old Post Office/General Store building which sits near the highway front area. There are two very old tombstone markers lying on the floor in there, which could explain why the activity is in that building. One of our investigators Harvey Martinez asked the question while looking down at one of the old cemetery tombstone markers. He asked "Is your name Mayfield?" and "Were you the one born on April 30, 1838?" I was recording this session at the time with both a full-spectrum video camera in one hand and my digital audio recorder in the other hand as he asked these questions. Later upon examining, it was determined that we picked up the very clear Class A EVP voice of an older man with a southern drawl accent saying "Yes". We have this video of that clear sounding EVP reply and other very good solid paranormal evidence videos on our popular YouTube channel "Seeking The Real Paranormal Truth...." where we share as much of our paranormal discoveries as we can with the public world. Our paranormal group/team has now had many paranormal investigations over time in Helena, Texas due to everything we have found and keep on discovering there both from historical and paranormal perspectives.

When we are asked by people of our opinions of the old Helena, Texas ghost town and if we think there is something very strange and unnatural going on there, our answer is quite simply……yes. In my own personal opinion, do I find that the paranormal activity there is extreme at times for unknown reasons? The answer to this question again is yes. Do I and our experienced paranormal team group Graveyard Shift Paranormal Investigations feel that this ghost town is truly mysterious and haunted. The answer to this question is again without any doubt……a very clear yes. There are just too many very strange unexplained and extreme ghostly situations, stories, and encounters by regular every day people visiting, other paranormal world people investigating, and also our own very solid paranormal evidence collected to not believe otherwise.

Old Helena Texas

Chapter 4: Victoria's Black Swan Inn (San Antonio, Texas)

Photo By: Dan LaFave

There are not many people who have not already heard about Victoria's Black Swan Inn located deep within the heart of San Antonio, Texas sitting on a majestic and beautiful 35 acres at 1006 Holbrook Road nestled and hidden between Rittiman and Eisenhauer roads not too far from Fort Sam Houston. I came to know of the Black Swan Inn several years ago upon being born and raised in San Antonio. Back in the early 1990's, I had a good friend get married out on the property where many grand and remembered weddings take place. I also remember having a great time that day for the wedding that lasted into the late hours of the night with partying and celebration. As people left throughout the evening, I found myself walking by myself throughout the grounds and house looking at everything and thinking what a neat place this really was. If you personally have never seen it, you need to. While I was walking around, I suddenly had the feeling that I was not alone.

I found myself inside the main parlor of the house where the baby grand piano sits, turning around many times and looking behind because I felt a very strong sense of being watched. This did not feel like an ominous sense, but at the same time it felt very strange to me. I could not put my finger on the feeling at the time, but I personally knew something was not right. In the late 1990's, I finally had the pleasure of meeting the owner, Jo Ann Rivera, of Victoria's Black Swan Inn. This friendship has gone on throughout the years to this day in 2013 and I also met her partner Phil Ross as well as Angelka Rogers along the way. We have all become good friends over time because of The Black Swan Inn and the paranormal world.

How we initially met was through me initially beginning to investigate the very strange paranormal encounters and stories that I had come to read about as to The Black Swan. I had developed in interest at this time due to strong paranormal encounters I sometimes personally had in other historic locations throughout Texas. I found myself around this time locating and reading up on locations with strong reported paranormal phenomenon occurring.

When I had come across a newspaper article and some other information about The Black Swan, I suddenly remembered back to that night several years before when I was walking around that property and felt those very strange sensations of being watched. That was when the realization occurred to me that maybe I was not imagining that feeling many years ago while walking around. Maybe something was reaching out to me trying to communicate or maybe it was simply watching me because it was curious. These were all questions that I had at that moment as I looked up as much information as I could about the history of The Black Swan Inn.

Photo By: Dan LaFave

This was around the time that I was beginning to take the paranormal world very seriously not just as a new found hobby, but much more. I would on occasion join some other paranormal enthusiastic people in small groups and we would stay overnight by paying a small fee. I felt that this small fee was a donation as to helping preserve the historical and beauty of the house and other buildings on the grounds. I also found at the time many years ago that Jo Ann was just so nice and friendly. She would want to sit down and share her many haunting stories as to living in the house on the old historic Victoria's Black Swan Inn property. I found these many ghostly haunting stories to be very fascinating and could just sit for hours listening to Jo and other people tell them. I knew way back then that the paranormal was much more than just a hobby to me; it was a very deep passion in which I needed to learn a whole lot more.

I found myself taking in as much of the historical information as I could and trying to match it to possible ghostly haunting things that were occurring. Jo Rivera would also during these late night paranormal investigation excursions put out the best platters of food and drinks for us to have and make sure that we were all okay and doing well. She has always made me feel so very welcome and that simply is the type of friendly and honest person she has always been as long as I have known her which has been a long time. The same can be said of our good friends Phil Ross (also owner of Yorktown Hospital) and Angelka Rogers (who does many things at both The Black Swan Inn and Yorktown Hospital).

Upon starting one of my first paranormal investigations at Victoria's Black Swan Inn many years ago, I really did not know what exactly to expect. I remember my first feeling there of great anticipation but also a lot of wariness. This again is a very large historical property with many buildings on it and is very spooky at night walking around it......especially alone. Upon walking in the main front downstairs parlor area, a person really feels like they have stepped back in time. They have done just a great job of preserving the beauty and historical restoration of this grand old house built back in 1867.

Photo By: Dan LaFave

The house and property also was once where the 1842 Battle Of The Salado took place. There is a historical marker that sits just off the main property where any person can see and read exactly what took place back in history.

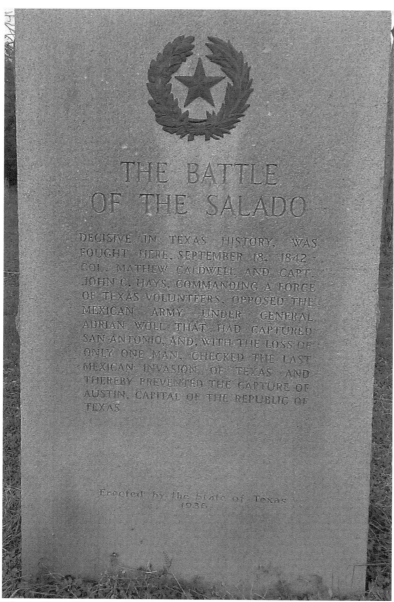

Photo By: Dan LaFave

During this decisive battle on September 18, 1842 that not too many know about from history books, a force of Texas volunteers commanded by Colonel Mathew Caldwell and Captain John C. Hays, stopped the last Texas invasion by defeating General Adrian Woll, commander of the Mexican army. This battle and defeat was accomplished by the miraculous result of only losing one man.

Back in those days, I was using a simple analog tape recorder, point and read infra-red thermometer, and black EMF meter (the exact same one that was later shown being used on the hit show Ghost Hunters on the SyFy Network). Everyone seemed to want that EMF detector after it was shown the first time on television, it is a very good meter. The digital audio recorders really had not really come around then and the available digital models were much more expensive than they are these days. I found back in those days that an analog tape recorder could pick up many great EVP's also and usually did. A person just had to get a model that did not create a lot of inside mechanical noise on the tape and more analyzing was needed to rule things out as to that.

As I started out on one of my first paranormal investigations of the Black Swan Inn, there was maybe a small group of 5 to 6 people who had come out this particular Friday or Saturday night. The weather and temperature were perfect around 80 degrees allowing us to keep the actual front door of the main house open. The plan was that if any of us became sleepy throughout the night that they would bed down in sleeping bags on the floor with a pillow in that main area. We had started to walk outside together taking pictures and doing recordings to see what and if we would get anything. We had something fascinating occur to us.

Photo By: Dan LaFave

We saw something really big and black sitting on one of the poles outside near the parking lot moving a little and looking at us. We were about 50 to 100 feet away when we first saw it. As we started to walk closer, this big black thing suddenly took flight and came right at us as if in attack mode or something. Two of the women screamed as this occurred and we all ducked as it almost went right over our heads making us jump. One of the guys in the group managed to snap a bunch of digital pictures of this event as it came up to us and when it went away. The very strange thing is that as it went by us, it seemed to vaporize and disappear into nothing.

We were asking ourselves if it went into the trees or bushes, but could not find anything upon our observation. When the guy started looking at his pictures, he yelled and told us all to come over and look. In looking at the pictures he had gotten, I could see that he managed to get about 4 pictures of this strange event. The first picture was this thing sitting on the pole right before it took flight to come right at us. In this picture, a person could clearly see the red eyes and strange shape that it had as it looked at us. In the second picture, it had started flight and we could see the huge wing span as it approached us.

Was this an owl which so many people see at night? That was a question that I started to lead to. In the third picture, it had passed us a little and could see that this thing seemed to resemble something other than a bird or owl except that it was red in color. It just did not seem to have the characteristics of being one and it was huge. It also had its head turned towards us in the picture and could see the very big red eyes of this thing from that picture. In the fourth picture, the mysterious thing was approximately 20 feet away by this time and this is the picture that really got us. In the picture, he captured this very strange entity vaporizing into nothing. There was a huge red color of what looked like an aura glow about it, and the entity was vaporizing and disappearing right into this red glow. All the pictures were very clear as well, anyone could see that there was no distortion caused by the camera. This was also the moment that we all witnessed with our own eyes this thing disappearing. What did we all see? Was this a bird or owl? Where did it go? Why couldn't we find it after it disappeared only a few feet from us? Why did this thing fly right at us as if in attack mode? Why didn't this thing look like a real owl or bird of prey that I had seen many times before at night flying? These were all questions that I had as I gathered my thoughts and tried to settle back down from the event. Things like this are very perplexing to say the least because of the rational thought that goes into trying to explain these strange events.

Photo By: Dan LaFave

As I investigated different parts of the house and buildings on the grounds, I eventually split off from the group who seemed to be doing their own thing and experiments. I had my Sony nightshot Mini-DV camcorder (which was very expensive and sophisticated for that time period many years ago) in my hand as I went room by room inside exploring to see what I could see. I saw through the window the other small group of people walking off down the sidewalk towards the garden area down the lawn. The house again was very dark and hard to see to the natural eye. I was having to use the viewfinder to the video camera with the infra-red mode on as to being able to see in the right side hallway wing and room area.

As I went around the corner looking in the viewfinder into one of the rooms, I suddenly found myself staring at 3 to 5 very large antique old dolls that were arranged in the room in the corner by an antique couch. One of these old dolls was large and very tall in height. Earlier in the night while walking around with the lights on, I did not remember seeing or noticing these dolls that I was now looking at. At least I did not pay much attention to them. Now, they were looking right back at me through that infra-red camcorder viewfinder. I remember hitting the focus a few times to get a better look at them and panned the whole room and then back to the largest doll. Every time I took the camera away from my eyes, I could not see. As I zoomed in on the doll's eyes, I could swear that they moved to look at me, the eyes also appeared to blink.

I kept focusing trying to see this again and filmed their exact positioning as I was doing so. After a minute of doing this, I heard a movement noise out in the hallway behind me that startled me. I turned around with the camera and shot into the hallway around the corner trying to see what had made that noise. I saw that the other people were still outside. I even took the camera away from my eyes to see with my own eyes, but it was much too dark. I could not see anything. I then heard another movement noise back inside the room to my left. When I turned and shot the camera and viewfinder back at the dolls, I suddenly saw something that really made my hair stand up. Right in front of me, the dolls had changed position as if someone or something had moved them. The heads were turned differently and the arms/legs all looked to be changed from their original positioning. It for sure looked to me like they had moved.

As I zoomed in on them trying to see, I focused the camera viewfinder again on the largest doll zooming in real close to those eyes. The dolls head was turned to the left sort of facing away from me now. As I focused in really close on it, the dolls head suddenly turned and looked directly towards me. I just about dropped the camcorder when that happened and turned and headed immediately outside in total shock, fear, and disbelief. Did I see what I just saw? In looking back at my video tape then, I realized that I had and also showed the rest of the group who stood there in shock. I unfortunately lost that video tape over the years and kicked myself for doing so. To this day, I still remember the way those doll's eyes looked at me as if it was alive.

During the rest of the night, everyone eventually went to sleep around 2:30am, except me. I found myself the only person awake in the house and on the property. Every time I heard a creak of the old wood or something settling, I turned around quickly because very old homes do this. I decided to do an experiment in the far left wing of the house. This was the wing where many people had extreme experiences with a closet there, including the owner Jo Ann Rivera. She had mentioned to me that on one occasion upon buying and moving into the home, she had gone to the closet one night to put a box up on the shelf. She had the light off as she did so with just the light from the hallway coming in. As she opened the door, she states that a pair of bright glowing blinking eyes was looking down right at her from that shelf area in the closet darkness. She states she could see this very clearly and really freaked her out where she nearly dropped the box she was holding and closed that door very quickly going back into the other room to try to regain her composure.

As I walked back into that dark very quiet room by myself, I remember Jo previously telling me that scary encounter/story. I also remember seeing the look in her eyes when she told me the story. Here I was walking around in the dark with my analog tape recorder and EMF meter about to do a paranormal experiment with everyone else asleep in the house. As I walked on the hard wood floor, I could hear the boards creak. I realized that if anyone were moving about, I could easily hear the boards creak to know that it was possibly a person moving about.

I went to one of the circular wood tables with 4 chairs around it and placed my analog tape recorder with dynamic microphone attached to it. The dynamic microphone enabled the machine to better and more clearly pick up any outside noise. I sat the microphone on its stand on the table and hit the red record button on the recorder. I then said out loud that I was leaving now and that I had put the tape recorder here for them to communicate and talk if they wanted to. I then walked quietly out of the room down the hallway to the other far wing of the building and sat down. I could see that the other people were all still in a deep sleep on the floor in the main room and that all was very quiet. I sat there a for about 5 to 10 minutes before deciding to go outside and walk around in the late night air to see if could see anything out there.

Upon coming back into the main house about thirty minutes later, I could see again that everyone was deeply asleep by then which was about 3 am. I carefully and very quietly again walked slowly back down the left hallway wing to the far left main room where I had put the analog tape recorder. I walked into the room feeling different, as if something were there with me. Something unseen seemed to fill the air around me. I sat down in the wooden chair there at the table with my headphones in hand and started to rewind and listen to the tape. At the beginning of the tape, I could hear just myself setting up everything and the old wooden floor boards creaking every time that I moved.

On the tape, the creaking of the wood sounded loud where there was no way that a person could move about in that room or the hallway without being detected by the recorder. This table was also placed near one of the corners several feet away from any open doorway. As I was listening, I could hear myself setting this recorder and microphone up and then stating that phrase that I said earlier. I then could myself turning and walking across the room and all the way down that long hallway towards the front of the house, with each step I took creaking on the old wooden floor boards. Then there was silence. Silence for approximately 4 to 5 minutes. That eerie silence deep within the night that we as paranormal investigators hear when we know no human being is present in that room or environment.

I was beginning to think nothing was going to happen. That is when I began to hear it. Was it a shuffle or a movement? As I continued to listen to the tape with my headphones, I heard the movement noise again, this time right up on the microphone. Then the microphone tapped just like someone tapping on a microphone with their finger. There again was that very eerie silence in between each movement noise. Suddenly the wooden chair pulled out from the table. What the hell was I hearing here? My thoughts raced at that moment. Did one of the other people come back into this room while I was outside? I then remembered again that there was no way any person could have walked down the hallway or even moved on this wooden floor without hearing them coming in as to the creaking of the wood boards.

Then it dawned upon me while listening to this, there was no creaking wood board sounds on the tape in between the movement noises that I was hearing and even when the chair was pulled out a little from under the table. Any person within the room trying to play around would have made noises because that is just human nature even in trying to make the most complex paranormal trick or hoax. At times, I could hear things being moved on the table, I believe there was a candle setting there. A few times, I thought that I could hear a little girl's voice mutter or say something, but it was faint. The movement noises however were very loud and made me jump each time I heard them. This went on for the whole 30 minute period while I was away in the other part of the house and outside.

At one point after that 30 minute period, I could hear myself coming back down the hallway creaking loudly on those wooden floor boards which got a lot louder the closer I got to the table and tape recorder microphone. In hearing this sound, it confirmed to me again that there was simply no way that any human person or animal could have been making these noises. Over that span of 30 minutes, this unseen presence moved about the room making noises and then would come back to the table. It tapped and played with the microphone several times almost knocking the microphone over at one point. The big thing again was that there simply was no footstep wooden board creaking sounds in between all those movement noises. This all simply amazed and intrigued me to want to learn a lot more about the paranormal ghostly world and all the happenings and history at Victoria's Black Swan Inn.

As to the history of the Black Swan Inn and all of the previous owners, it really is very interesting to review and look at. It is said that the land that the Black Swan Inn sits on was once the land of Native American Indians on Salado Creek thousands of years ago. There have been different old stone tool artifacts and arrowheads found all throughout the property. The area is very green and lush, and a person could easily imagine ancient Indian tribes living their lives on this land. At one time, Heinrich (Henry) Mahler and his wife Marie Biermann Mahler, emigrated in the 1800's from Germany shortly after their marriage. They proceeded to purchase 200 acres of land where they built what was their original first homestead.

Back in those days, many settlers purchased as much land as they could, and Mahler later purchased more land where they built a newer house on a hill overlooking Salado Creek which they later moved into. It appears that Henry Mahler had many ranching and farming interests, but his main focus at the time seemed to be in dairy farming. For many years, he worked hard and he and Marie had four children. Marie died at the age of 73 in 1923 and Henry died at the age of 83 a few years after his wife's passing. According to records, it appears that the much of the property there on the Salado Creek was left to two sons, Daniel and Sam, who split it up amongst themselves. The Mahler farms and homestead were sold about a decade later.

The land and main original house were then bought by the Holbrook family, but which the road there is now called. This is when modifications were made by them to what is now what the main house looks like. Two long wings with adjoining rooms were added on both sides of the older house as well as a back kitchen area. A grand looking front porch was also remodeled. This all made the house as big as it is today with its many rooms and large square footage. They had some good friends, by the last name of Woods, who also lived there with them. It is said that the Holbrooks had no children of their own unfortunately, but the daughter of their friends, Joline Woods, eventually lived in the house and married an attorney by the name of Hall Park Street Jr. who was very prominent within San Antonio at the time.

After the death of her father, Joline's mother Blanche lived in the house with them. It appears that this was the time that the second floor addition was made to the house in order to accommodate more people living there since the Streets had children of their own.

It seemed that their family had many fun times and social gatherings on the house and property. It also appeared there was a lot of tragedy to also take place on the property. Young Joline Woods was to die a very untimely death by cancer. The attorney Park Street went on to remarry later and both he and his later wife lived in the house for years afterwards the death of his first wife. Things again took another very tragic and gruesome turn when his body was found by his wife on August 4, 1965. He had apparently been having some possible financial, business, and mental problems and had committed suicide by hanging inside the house. The home and property over the years went on as to changing hands and owners over the years till it was bought by Jo Ann Rivera.

Photo By: Dan LaFave

Over the years, the haunting ghostly activity began that included hearing mysterious music playing from an unknown source or from the piano downstairs, people seeing and witnessing very solid different ghostly apparitions standing and watching in the house or on the grounds only to quickly disappear after being seen, apparitions looking through upstairs windows at night from outside. Sometimes loud walking footsteps and other noises will be heard all throughout the house during both the day and night. Doors will mysteriously close and lock by themselves unable to be opened only to be found wide open and unlocked later.

Very strange odors will manifest in the air as to decay or perfume scents that would appear and then disappear quickly. Apparitions of children are seen and captured by both camera and video camcorder within in the house and on the stairs. Audible loud voices are heard calling out to someone when no one is there, sometimes by name. A hostile ghostly male spirit believed to be that of Henry (original owner) in the old milk barn behind the main house who appears to hate men and confronting them. There are also many ghostly very clear EVP (electronic voice phenomenon) recordings by people and paranormal investigators stating sometimes chilling and other times friendly welcoming phrases.

There is also a very friendly little spirit girl by the name of Sara who makes herself known to many people in various ways of communication. She appears to be very young but knows as to what is happening or being asked of her to do. The evidence is there. One of the scariest encounters and stories I have heard over time was that of a plumber who crawled under the house one day as to working on the pipes. He heard a noise behind him and turned to see the ghostly apparitions of several crouched Indians under there looking at him. It is said that he left the house and property in a hurry.

Victoria's Black Swan Inn in San Antonio, Texas is again a very beautiful historic location with a lot of confirmed solid paranormal activity. It also is a great place to have weddings or professional pictures taken. Is this house and property haunted? I and many other very experienced credible paranormal researchers have found a lot of very strong confirmed paranormal activity evidence there and believe that it is one of the most haunted active locations in San Antonio and all of Texas.

Do we know exactly why all the paranormal activity and ghostly spirits are there? Do we know all the real stories of what possibly took place? No, can't say as paranormal researchers that we do for sure at this time, but it does appear that some of those personal haunting experiences are welcoming while some are not. People have had strong ghostly encounters that includes the filming production crew of a famous country music star while filming a past music video segment inside the main house where strange things happened. What I can say is if you want to have a possible true real haunting experience and you are in the San Antonio area, be sure that you contact Victoria's Black Swan Inn directly either online or by phone and speak with my good friends Jo Ann Rivera, Phil Ross, or Angelka Rogers and they will give you the full history, stories, and even take you on a scheduled nightly ghost hunt during one of their tours of the house and property. San Antonio, Texas is also regarded in the top ten lists of America's most haunted cities and Victoria's Black Swan Inn is one of the reasons. Who knows, chances might be really good that you will have that haunted ghostly experience you are looking for.

Chapter 5: Presidio La Bahia
(Goliad, Texas)

Photo By: Dan LaFave

Several years ago around 2004, I had the pleasure of exploring and doing paranormal research for the first time at Presidio La Bahia located in Goliad, Texas. While the lead paranormal investigator on a San Antonio, Texas based paranormal team, I had personally looked at and researched many ghostly stories and encounters by people who had either worked at or visited Presidio La Bahia before. I discovered at that time that there were stories ranging from very extreme haunted ghostly experiences to some experiences that possibly could just be a myth or urban legend as many people call them. I had told the founder of this team that I was very interested and was going to personally rent The Quarters at Presidio La Bahia so that this whole other paranormal team including that founder could have an opportunity to investigate this location for the very first time.

It seemed from what I found that there was a lot of great relatively unknown Texas history here and unexplainable ghostly stories that evolved from this old Spanish garrison through newspaper stories. This truly looked to be a remarkable historical as well as possible paranormal location. The stories were not really explored in those days, because nothing had really been confirmed or proven there yet by credible paranormal teams as to paranormal activity. My personal goal at the time was to go in to see what exactly I and the rest of this paranormal team would find. I could not at that time find any recorded instances of credible paranormal research teams actually going in and spending the whole night researching to see what they would find or discover there.

In looking at everything, I contacted the museum there at Presidio La Bahia and reserved The Quarters for our first nightly paranormal investigation there. Some people in the group had to rent motel rooms within the nearly town of Goliad, Texas to stay in.

Photo By: Dan LaFave

In making the vehicle trip from San Antonio, Texas to Goliad, Texas which is almost two hours on the highway, I discovered that Presidio La Bahia was an awesome place to drive up to. You find yourself going down the highway looking for the signs as to it, and then suddenly.....there it is. It is a pretty big Texas historic location and hard to miss. It also takes on an ominous look and feel to it at night.

Photo By: Dan LaFave

Upon unloading everything, I decided to take a tour of the museum there to get a good feel as to the history of the old Spanish garrison. Other members of the paranormal group were going all over taking as many pictures of things as they could. The excitement of being there could clearly be seen in everyone's faces. I was glad that I took the time to find it and look at all of the history there which was extreme to say the least. Many people do not know that history and how brutal it really was for the Texas soldier prisoners who died there.

Originally this fort was established by the Spanish in 1721 on the ruins of an old French fort near Lavaca Bay, Texas thus being where this old Spanish garrison got the name 'La Bahia' which is Spanish for 'the bay'. The Spanish ended up moving this fort garrison a few times for strategic Texas land territory control reasons and this fort was later firmly established around 1749 on the banks of the

San Antonio River just within the city limits of present day Goliad. There were outer camp settlements that sprung up around this old fort that formed what Goliad, Texas is today. This presidio at the time was also one of the main Spanish garrisons controlling much of what are the eastern and coastal regions of Texas. When Mexico later obtained independence from Spain, this presidio became one of their major defensive position garrisons.

Settlers all over Texas around this time were tired of having first been under strict Spanish control, and now were under even stricter control from Mexico. Texas settlers began to get together, talk, and devise ways of trying to establish their independence and freedom from Mexico. A group of brave Texas soldiers under the command of Colonel George Collingsworth in 1835 were able during a battle/skirmish to obtain total control of the Presidio La Bahia outpost from the Spanish. Also, believe it or not, the first Declaration of Texas Independence was signed at the fort a few months later in December of 1835. A vicious, ruthless Mexican dictator was arising to great power around that same time.......General Antonio Lopez de Santa Anna.

Presidio La Bahia was put under the command of Colonel James Walker Fannin with a sizeable group of Texas defenders. This would only prove to be a short time because this particular Presidio seemed to change hands quite a few times because of its strategic defensive positioning and location within the old Texas frontier. They also had no way to foresee what horrible things would later happen to them all. Colonel Fannin I am sure never thought at the time that his name would be written in history the way it was. Am sure he also did not foresee the fate that was to await both he and the men under his command.

Colonel Fannin was born in Georgia and later attended the United States Military Academy at Westpoint, but did not graduate as to grades. He then became a merchant before ending up in the Texas territory owning a plantation. He and many others really resented being under the control of the very harsh Mexican government in Texas.

This did not apparently sit well at all with General Santa Anna because he assembled and put together a very large conquering Mexican army and headed north towards San Antonio, Texas which is really not far from Goliad to take control of another very important famous fort/garrison called The Alamo. Many in the Mexican territory had heard what a tyrant Santa Anna was, but no one really had any idea until they faced him. A lot of very sinister unjust brutal things were taking place in old Texas around this time of history. Many people who know about Texas history only seem to really focus on The Alamo as if that was the only Texas history, but there seemed to be a chain reaction of very dark ruthless things taking place at the time in the Central Texas and Gulf Coast regions.

During a very vicious and brutal thirteen day siege and assault of The Alamo by General Santa Anna and his 1500 troops between the dates of February 23rd to March 6th 1836, a very brave Texas force of defenders led by commanders James Bowie and William B. Travis along with many other Texas volunteers including Davy Crockett held their own the best that they could before The Alamo fell finally with the deaths of approximately 600 men. Nearly all of the Texas men defenders were killed and it is said that General Santa Anna even ordered the executions by sword of any Texas male defenders by who had actually surrendered during the battle. Gen. Santa Anna was spreading a message to the rest of the Texas resistance and that message was that he was not done.

Santa Anna had also dispatched another force of Mexican soldiers under the command of General Jose de Urrea to head up the Texas coastline as to capturing Presidio La Bahia. This not much heard about battle took place a few weeks later on March 19 and 20, 1836. It was called the Battle of Coleto Creek. Colonel James Fannin had earlier taken his men out away from Presidio La Bahia after receiving word from Colonel Travis in his attempt to head up towards San Antonio as to trying to help defend and fight at The Alamo. In those days, it took a band of defenders/soldiers several days and weeks of marching and setting up camp to make the journeys that now are very quick by vehicle. Word of things also took time, especially if there were no survivors to help spread that word. It is thought that he had possibly received orders from Sam Houston to fall back due to what occurred at The Alamo and also give up the presidio fort to the advancing large Mexican army.

When he and his men decided to retreat to a better defensive position towards Victoria, Texas, they were caught suddenly off guard near Coleto Creek while retreating eastward by the Mexican force led by General Urrea. The Texas defenders formed a square in their valiant defense because they were attacked at the same time from several different directions at once by the Mexican army and had no cover by which to protect themselves. There was nothing the Texas defenders could do due to the fact that they were surprised and outnumbered here. They were eventually taken prisoner.

All of the soldiers who survived were led back to Presidio La Bahia where they were held under guard as prisoners of war. They were taken out into the fields for daily work excursions and made to do hard work and things for the Mexican soldiers at the garrison. They were also treated very harshly and brutally. It is said that the wounded soldiers from the battle at the creek were not looked after very well and were suffering within the presidio. Little did those Texas defenders know as to what gruesome atrocity was to await them. This Palm Sunday was not going to be like the rest for them. The Mexican government wanted to send another very harsh as to the Texas resistance. They wanted every Texas resistance fighter to know what it as like to fight the great Mexican empire as Santa Anna referred to it. The Mexican government wanted everyone living there to know that this whole land and territory that so many settlers had come to and called the new Republic of Texas at that time was still Mexico.

On that fateful early morning, Colonel Fannin and his men thought that it was just going to be another day. Did they know and have an idea of what was going to happen? A person can only imagine how they felt at that time. Later that early morning on March 27, 1836, it was discovered what General Santa Anna had ordered. The Texas defenders were led out of Presidio La Bahia in groups, and some along with the wounded were left behind at the garrison. Colonel James Fannin was kept in different quarters than the rest of his men for those days held captive in the garrison. He was kept in a room inside and to the right rear side of Chapel of our Lady of Loreto which sits within the presidio grounds. Orders were given to Colonel Portilla to commit the act. General Santa Anna had ruthlessly ordered the execution and deaths of 342 men. This number is twice as many men who died while defending The Alamo a few weeks earlier.

The fact is that these Texas defenders and prisoners were not only wrongly executed, but their remains were desecrated. It is said that one group was executed about a quarter of a mile on San Antonio Road, another group on Copano Road, and the third group on Victoria Road. They were marched to these locations and without warning the Mexican soldiers filed rank and fired upon all the unarmed Texas defender prisoners killing everyone. It is said that the Mexican soldiers then went back to the presidio and killed most of the wounded (39 Texas soldiers) in the same brutal fashion.

The harshest and cruel event is what occurred to Colonel Fannin who was left last as to being executed. He made a simple reply after being led from his captive room inside the grounds of Presidio La Bahia to the front of the chapel after having first witnessing his brave Texas men being killed. They blindfolded him. He then spoke and made three respectful prisoner requests of the Mexican command. He asked first for all his personal possessions to please be sent to his family. He then asked to not be shot in the face. His last request was that he be given a Christian rightful burial. The Mexican soldiers than shot him in the face and burned his body just like all the other Texas defender bodies that that were piled, burned, and left on the ground in different areas both inside and outside Presidio La Bahia. The Mexican soldiers than stole and took all of Colonel James Fannin's possessions. It is said that a couple weeks or so passed before other Texas defenders who made it to Presidio La Bahia discovered the atrocity and all the burned mutilated dead bodies all over. It must have been a very shocking seen for anyone. They did what they could as to gathering and burying the dead in the best manner possible in an area behind the modern Presidio La Bahia.

A person in modern times can only imagine what the rest of the new Texas territory and the United States felt upon hearing the very gruesome events that took place first at The Alamo and then of the even more horrific tragic event that took place at Presidio La Bahia. General Sam Houston and his Texas defender forces sure felt it. They must of screamed very loudly when they rallied and shrieked "Remember The Alamo" and "Remember Goliad and Presidio La Bahia" when they avenged all those deaths and defeated General Antonio Lopez de Santa Anna at the battle site of San Jacinto a few weeks later on April 21, 1836 thus winning ultimate and complete Texas independence from Mexico.

As I deeply thought to myself upon arriving and looking at Presidio La Bahia and the chapel as to my very first visit there that afternoon, I thought about all of the brutal and harsh events that took place long ago where I was standing. In walking throughout the museum there and looking at all the very old genuine artifacts and pictures, I tried to imagine all the pain and suffering that took place right here at this very majestic historical location that my eyes were now focused upon. Many of us live our lives full of happiness and prosperity, while other brave individuals sometimes die very tragic deaths for what they believe in.......freedom and independence from some dark power trying to dominate them.

I thought to myself this was exactly how all of these very brave Texas defenders died. They died as to trying to gain their Texas independence from Mexico. They believed in the Republic of Texas. I tried to think what might have been going through their heads in history so long ago at this very location. Did they have the chance to make their last wishes in thought towards their families? Did they know that they were all about to die such an atrocious brutal death by the hands of a ruthless dictator? Did they know if their souls were worthy as to passing on towards the light to a better place or were some of their souls doomed to some unknown purgatory within Presidio La Bahia and on the grounds all around it?

Photo By: Dan LaFave (Fannin Memorial)

A memorial that is located behind Presidio La Bahia to the right side was erected and dedicated in 1938 by the state of Texas in honor of Col. James Fannin and the many other Texas defenders that gave their lives 1938. This very grand monument is also a very large mass grave of the many burned and charred remains of those long ago brave Texas defenders was declared a historical site as well.

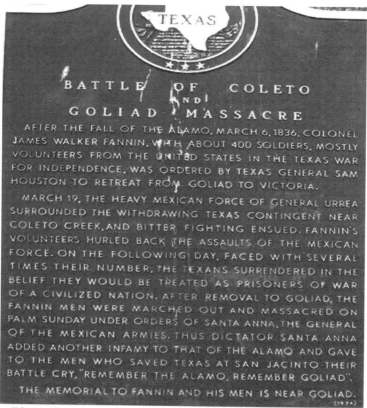

TEXAS

BATTLE OF COLETO
AND
GOLIAD MASSACRE

AFTER THE FALL OF THE ALAMO, MARCH 6, 1836, COLONEL
JAMES WALKER FANNIN, WITH ABOUT 400 SOLDIERS, MOSTLY
VOLUNTEERS FROM THE UNITED STATES IN THE TEXAS WAR
FOR INDEPENDENCE, WAS ORDERED BY TEXAS GENERAL SAM
HOUSTON TO RETREAT FROM GOLIAD TO VICTORIA.

MARCH 19, THE HEAVY MEXICAN FORCE OF GENERAL URREA
SURROUNDED THE WITHDRAWING TEXAS CONTINGENT NEAR
COLETO CREEK, AND BITTER FIGHTING ENSUED. FANNIN'S
VOLUNTEERS HURLED BACK THE ASSAULTS OF THE MEXICAN
FORCE. ON THE FOLLOWING DAY, FACED WITH SEVERAL
TIMES THEIR NUMBER, THE TEXANS SURRENDERED IN THE
BELIEF THEY WOULD BE TREATED AS PRISONERS OF WAR
OF A CIVILIZED NATION. AFTER REMOVAL TO GOLIAD, THE
FANNIN MEN WERE MARCHED OUT AND MASSACRED ON
PALM SUNDAY UNDER ORDERS OF SANTA ANNA, THE GENERAL
OF THE MEXICAN ARMIES. THUS DICTATOR SANTA ANNA
ADDED ANOTHER INFAMY TO THAT OF THE ALAMO AND GAVE
TO THE MEN WHO SAVED TEXAS AT SAN JACINTO THEIR
BATTLE CRY, "REMEMBER THE ALAMO, REMEMBER GOLIAD".

THE MEMORIAL TO FANNIN AND HIS MEN IS NEAR GOLIAD.
(1971)

Photo By: Dan LaFave

A person can walk behind Presidio La Bahia like I have done many times and read the inscriptions on that mass burial marker as to all the names of the men who lost their lives. To again think in a paranormal historical sense that so many men lost their lives on that very fateful tragic day. In those days, things like this were really felt and still are. Those many men along with Col. William Fannin fought and defended for what they believed in and stood for. They truly sacrificed their blood and souls for what they believed in.

All of these deep emotional feelings resounded over and over within my head as I as a paranormal researcher led and got the investigative group going. Standing at the memorial earlier that day, I had gotten down on my knees and bowed my head in prayer at one point, and could feel tears developing in sadness as I read about that history and saw those many names of the deceased inscribed on that monument. When a person is truly Texas born and raised such as me, they understand these feelings much better because they want to know what that sometimes ruthless Texas history was like for so many people in those days.

Upon starting the investigation and walking around Presidio La Bahia a lot more, I soon discovered different things upon taking many pictures as I fully documented this paranormal investigation. To the far right front side, there was a cannon sitting high up on its perch overlooking the front basin area of the presidio. This presidio the way it now looks is very different than it looked way back then. Thanks to a large donation of money and dedication by philanthropist Kathryn O'Connor in the 1960's, a very big restoration project of Presidio La Bahia took place as to the way it looks today when a person sees it.

Some things have changed in history from what this presidio looked like back then, very much like how The Alamo also was changed from the way that it originally looked. A person upon really looking at history and looking at really old pictures or drawings of historical locations can see how they truly looked, but restoration projects especially in Texas do a very good job of trying to restore back to the original look based on what people envisioned. So many locations fall into ruin because of lack of funding and donations which is very sad. Over time, change does happen, but the true beauty, essence, and preserved authentic look is there at the presidio to give people a real idea. Walking around in there during the day, a person feels safe. Walking around in there at night, a person sometimes feels extreme sadness and fear. Looking at the old cannon high up on the corner guarded perch approximately 30 feet in the air on that wall when I snapped the picture reminded me again that Colonel James Walker Fannin and his men once considered this historical location a fort of dominance.

Photo By: Dan LaFave

There again are many ghostly stories and encounters by people at Presidio La Bahia. One of these detailed what seemed like extreme stories that I saw years ago was a newspaper account by a security guard that was working there one night. It seems that this security guard was working one night there at the presidio guarding and looking after things that had been put out for a special event that they were having. He was doing his checks and rounds of the presidio grounds very late into the night with nothing out of the ordinary occurring to him. When around midnight came, things began to take a turn towards the ghostly paranormal extreme for him.

He described that he first witnessed hearing ear piercing cries of sadness emanating from somewhere within the presidio grounds. He said that it sounded like children wailing as if in pain and agony. It appears that he walked all over inside trying to determine where these very strange cries and screams were coming from. Some experienced paranormal researchers know this, but there are many people who do not. There are many hidden unmarked graves inside Presidio La Bahia all along the front, side, and back wall areas of Chapel of our Lady of Lorento. There are men, women, and children buried in these many unmarked graves. Why these graves are unmarked is another mystery.

Photo By: Dan LaFave (Chapel of our Lady of Loreto)

As this security guard walked around trying to locate those wails and screams, he must have thought that he was going crazy. The fact is that he was not. Most experienced security guards are very rational logical and practical people.

They know how to reason things out as to their jobs, but this very strange unnatural supernatural event must have surely started to frighten him. He described the cries as being very loud coming out of the darkness at him. Finally, he determined where the screams and cries were coming.......from the chapel area. When a person is alone and experiencing things like this, that experience can be pretty scary and unnerving.

There are records that show the locations of these unmarked graves and a person these days can easily go online as to the internet and find the unmarked grave plot locations. All of this in fact shows that the inside of Presidio La Bahia in a lot of perspective is actually a cemetery even though it is not officially designated as a cemetery. In the days of past as to the atrocity and other deaths that took place, people essentially buried their families where they could, which was near or right up against any religious structure.

Photo By: Dan LaFave

This security guard must have again been thinking that he was losing his mind or that he was imagining things. Other people have had the same sort of supernatural experiences there at Presidio La Bahia.......as an experienced paranormal researcher, I certainly have. It is said that once he located the source or area of where the screams and crying came from, that they suddenly stopped as mysteriously as they began. Was it over? It was then that he heard a very strange choir type singing noise coming from the rear area and grounds inside Presidio La Bahia. He described it as sounding like women singing as if in church. The only problem is that the chapel there was locked up tight, and there was no one inside it that night. Around that same time, something very frightening began to occur that he claims to have witnessed.

After a little while, he then claimed that a very strange mist began to come out of and form on the ground right by the actual marked gravesite of Annie Taylor in front of the chapel who is said to have died at a very young age in 1852 due to complications from tuberculosis. He watched as this mist came out of the ground floating and swirling around till finally it formed into the figure of a woman. He described this ghostly female apparition figure as wearing a white dress which resembled a wedding gown. At this time, he was surely shocked and frightened by what was occurring by the locked front doors of the old chapel.

He also described this ghostly figure in detail as if she were moving about as if in search of something. He stated that she floated approximately two feet off the ground as this ghostly apparition moved about the area by the chapel. He must have then tried to get a better look at her, when he claims that this ghostly female apparition stopped, turned, and looked right at him with a look of surprise to match his own expression. Then the ghostly female apparition floated off towards the back area of Presidio La Bahia. He claims that it drifted over the back wall towards the old cemetery that is located behind the presidio. I myself have actually walked back to this old cemetery which is behind that back wall and saw all the old gravesite markers and dates way back when. I am sure that people buried in that cemetery have had a lot of connection with Presidio La Bahia.

There are also stories of the ghostly figure of a small monk or friar that is seen manifesting near the back area of the chapel and then walks back to where the old well is situated. It also appears as if he is looking for something unseen and it is said that this ghostly apparition seems to be chanting. It is also said that this spirit is responsive and aggressive upon being seen and encountered and will actually come towards anyone seeing it. To this day, no one knows why exactly there are sometimes ghostly encounters by people of hearing music, voices, singing, seeing ghostly apparitions from time to time, and hearing sounds of gunfire. I do know that I myself have obtained a lot of paranormal evidence while investigating at night within the presidio.

During that night's investigation, we split up into groups and did many EVP recording sessions and then listened immediately back to what we just had done. At first, there was nothing, but then things began to change. During one of the recording sessions, a male unknown Spanish sounding voice said the actual name of one of the people in our investigative group. This really astonished me. There were also other EVP's that suddenly appeared on my digital audio recorder, with even a clear ghostly EVP of a man with a southern accent responding "Yes" when I asked if Colonel James Walker Fannin was present and if he could hear me. This voice did not match any of the males within our paranormal investigative group.

There were also times while we were doing recording sessions inside The Quarters, that we could hear movement outside and at times there were responsive knocks within the room and on the door that leads to the inside of the presidio. We had the lights off while we were recording, with our EMF detectors on, and the detectors were spiking very high at times throughout the recorded EVP sessions. We also had some psychics within the group who were definitely picking up on and sensing Mexican soldiers in uniform around us at times.

Photo By: Dan LaFave (Inside The Quarters)

The psychics said that the soldiers were standing there watching at times and wondering what we were doing. They also said that the Mexican soldiers appeared hostile towards us as if they wanted us to leave. At one point while sitting during one of the recording sessions, I felt a very cold sensation come up directly behind me and then it was on my shoulder feeling as if someone had put their hand on my shoulder. I had my back towards the front door area and turned immediately to see what I was feeling. The psychics in the group were experiencing and feeling all sorts of things around us.

At that precise moment in the darkness, I saw what looked to me to be the outlined shadow figure shape of a Mexican uniformed soldier approximately six feet tall in the other small bedroom area walk quickly from the middle of the room right through the stone wall towards the inside of Presidio La Bahia area. The ghostly apparition was darker than the darkness around it; this is how I could see the outline. I knew it was a soldier because I could see the strange shape outline of what looked like an historic Mexican hat on his head. I had seen that hat shape in pictures in the museum earlier. I remember how I got up out of the chair in shock at that moment as to what I had just witnessed. I took many digital pictures at that moment, but obtained nothing in that particular room which was a very cold temperature. Remembering back, it looked and appeared to me that the ghostly apparition knew that I saw him, and that he was trying to evade being discovered. It seemed responsive and with intelligence.

During my paranormal investigations at Presidio La Bahia, I have had very strange ghostly paranormal encounters such as being touched, hearing voices calling out, seeing strange light anomalies with the naked eye, seeing strange light within the chapel at night........even heard the chapel bell ring late one night mysteriously. There have been times where my equipment has failed even though fully powered, and have gone through severe battery drainage for unknown reasons. I have also seen strange shapes in the courtyard late at night, but which were too far to really focus on by eye or video camcorder. By the time I would focus, it would be gone.

On misty cold nights, Presidio La Bahia seems to take on an even spookier feel and experience. Walking around on those nights, I definitely felt as if I was being watched from different areas of the courtyard by things unseen. At times I would also hear footsteps that sounded like boots following me. All the while, these instances would come and go. I have gotten very clear loud Class A EVP's from men, women, and children during those investigations in which some were in direct response to the questions being asked. I even picked up eerie strange music one time on a recording when I heard the music playing. I also like many others could not determine where exactly the music was coming from. At times, it seemed to be coming from inside the locked chapel. Other times it appeared to be coming from the courtyard area by the museum. There were also times that I thought I heard or saw what were kids climbing on the back wall, but when I got to the area, there was no one and it was pretty late at night when that happened.

Do I as an experienced paranormal researcher personally feel from all the history, the many ghostly stories/encounters by people, and all my very own paranormal encounters and evidence that Presidio La Bahia is haunted? Yes, I do. I also think that there are times here where that brutal harsh past crosses over into our time and existence. With the Goliad Massacre happening the way that it did, how could Presidio La Bahia not be haunted.

Photo By: Dan LaFave

Chapter 6: Myrtles Plantation (St. Francisville, Louisiana)

Photo By: Dan LaFave

For anyone who has ever investigated or has toured the Myrtles Plantation located in St. Francisville, Louisiana before, you will surely enjoy my very real and true paranormal adventures and encounters there. Even if you have never been there, please read and follow closely everything that I tell you.......and if you want a real very spooky ghostly experience, go there and stay the night! Chances are pretty high and good that you might possibly have that ghostly experience you are looking for.

This book so far has been primarily about my many haunted adventures and paranormal investigations at exciting spooky Texas historical locations, but there are some other very haunted places outside of Texas that I have had the pleasure of seeing and investigating. For any serious paranormal investigator/researcher, it takes a lot of time to get around to seeing and investigating different locations around the country and it unfortunately is very expensive to travel these days. In 2005, I finally had my chance to investigate the Myrtles Plantation after hearing and seeing all the haunted stories about it. The other thing is that I did not just investigate for one day and night like so many other people do upon their stays there. I investigated for 4 nights in a row there staying in a different room of The Myrtles Plantation main house each time. This was also during the week, which means it was very quiet and great for investigating.

The drive from Texas to St. Francisville, Louisiana was one of adventure and enthusiasm. It was a long drive, with most of it in Texas due to huge state size, but once I arrived in Louisiana heading towards Baton Rouge, I was really enjoying the scenery along Interstate 10. Most people who do not live in Texas or who have never ever lived in Texas have any idea how large the state of Texas really is. For those of you in the east or northeast regions of the United States, I will give you an idea. If you take Texas and plant it on the east coast somewhere, this state would swallow up at least 6 states. It takes an entire day of driving to get out of Texas if you are crossing it. Texas also due to its large size has just about every type of habitat and environment from desert like conditions to thick piney woods. Texas is a great state with a lot of very active paranormal locations both still undiscovered and discovered, but there are also many other great states that have awesome haunted locations for the person with an avid paranormal/supernatural interest as to new discovery.

Once a person enters Louisiana, and sees all the bayous, swamps, and Spanish moss there hanging from most of the trees, that person has a feeling that they have really stepped back into one of the oldest historical parts of the United States. Especially when driving across the section of Interstate 10 that crosses the Atchafalaya Swamp which is for many miles. My thought upon this literal many mile bridge highway over the swamp was.......please don't let my vehicle break down or have any mechanical problems here. It is also a very heavily traveled highway corridor as to traffic. There luckily are a lot of Louisiana Highway

Patrol officers patrolling up and down that section of the highway. Upon getting to Baton Rouge, and then swinging north towards St. Francisville, Louisiana and the Myrtles Plantation, I really started to notice how old and dated everything looked. It was like a long step back into history and time.

Now, what really surprised me was how hidden the Myrtles Plantation is. I almost missed it entirely on the highway if it were not for the highway signs on U.S. Highway 61 there in St. Francisville. The plantation if you have never seen in has a row of very thick trees totally shielding it from the highway there. I could not even see the main house from the highway as I pulled up to the main property. The main sign that greeted me there at the main entrance read....Circa 1796, The Myrtles Plantation, The Home Of Mystery And Intrigue. I wondered what it was like beyond that sign, because I could not see the main house yet upon turning right into the long driveway that wound past the old gatehouse and through the main garden.

104

As I drove through two very old big trees, I suddenly saw The Myrtles Plantation sitting there looking at me. It really is a beautiful place. I could not wait to park and get out of the car to start walking around taking more pictures of everything. I had read so many things about this place and even read the book "The Myrtles Plantation" written by Frances Kermeen. This was a very interesting book to me because the author actually bought and lived in The Myrtles Plantation for a decade many years ago and I read about her many ghostly haunted experiences there while living alone in this huge plantation house.

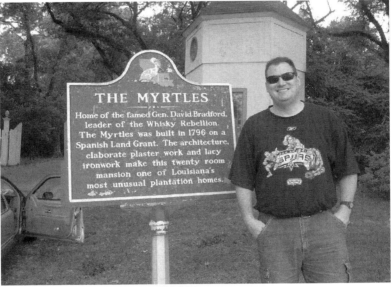

Photo By: Dan LaFave (2005)

I could not imagine what it might have felt like for her living in this big house all alone with all of the sometimes extreme paranormal activity. Living in a true haunted home can a lot of times drive people nuts, I have seen and witnessed many times what people go through when they experience extreme paranormal ghostly activity. It is an environment where literally anything can happen each day or night within a home. Imagine always feeling like you are being watched or preyed upon in your own home every time you are alone. That is the feeling that Frances must have felt while living in this plantation home built in 1796.

Photo By: Dan LaFave

As I parked the car in the parking lot to the left side of the main house and got out of the vehicle to get a really good look, I suddenly could see and feel something with this very old plantation home. After months of preparation and reading any article I could find as to history and ghostly experiences by people, I now finally in 2005 was going to have the opportunity as an experienced paranormal investigator/researcher to spend 4 nights in this very old plantation home staying 4 of the most documented haunted activity rooms to see what I would discover and find out for myself. It was time for me as an experienced researcher to see if the many haunting ghostly stories were real and had solid substance to them. I say this because it is so easy these days for false things to get out there in the world about possible haunted locations. In my opinion and also my wife Connie's opinion, it takes a lot for a place to be deemed haunted as the term implies.

I could not wait to go to the main office and get all checked in as to staying the very first day and night in the General David Bradford Suite on the first floor which has a large bedroom with a full poster full-size bed and an adjoining sitting room as well as two verandahs joining it as well. This was a very big suite type room and upon walking into it, I could feel things already. I just knew in the back of my mind that there was something or someone else there, even though I had not even started investigating yet. I got all unpacked and started to take as many pictures as I could of that room and the outside porch and garden areas. I was pretty excited to say the least, and could not wait for the sun to go down.

Photo By: Dan LaFave

That first day and night there at the old plantation was just going to be the beginning of things to happen.

Many people do not realize that even the most seasoned paranormal investigators/researchers always have a lot of fun and excitement as to exploring new possible locations with paranormal/supernatural activity in them. This world is never boring to say the least. It is the exact opposite feeling to us actually, because we usually are pretty psyched and ready to go into any new location when we arrive, because we have done a lot of personal research on that location already. The Myrtles Plantation was no different to me, because I felt like I already knew the place and history. As to the ghosts, I did not come to know them...........yet.

I signed up for one of the daily history tours, because I wanted to hear more before I started my personal paranormal investigation later that night. This was important to me in as to my visit and quest to the Myrtles Plantation for those 4 days and nights. I was there to try to confirm if the many stories were true or not from my own perspective after having done this on a high level for years.

Photo By: Dan LaFave

I found the tour through the main plantation house very interesting because it provided even more information for me. You see, very serious experienced paranormal investigators try to take as much information that they have and put that information into their paranormal investigations as to trying to confirm paranormal activity. We try to get answers to our questions as to who, what, when, how, and where. With this kind of historical information provided, that gives us the opportunity to bring many things together at once as to how we investigate and what exactly we are able to find out or confirm from that paranormal investigation. I found the story of the mirror in the main hallway interesting.

Photo By: Dan LaFave

The story goes that they believed in the past that mirrors were the windows to our souls and that if all the mirrors in a home were not covered upon someone passing as in death, then their soul instead of going to heaven would instead be trapped within the mirror as if in a purgatory. I had heard this story many times throughout the many different locations I had investigated throughout the South and this belief or superstition as to what some people call it seemed to be very strong in this Louisiana region.

Many superstitions and folklore stories as to the paranormal/supernatural are out there. Many are true, while others are just that......stories which get changed over time by people telling them. I do personally believe that mirrors have a lot to do with the paranormal because I have encountered very strange things with mirrors during investigations and I have heard many very strange encounters of people seeing ghostly things in mirrors as to reflection even though nothing is seen with naked eye standing there. Maybe mirrors truly are looking towards the other side as so many people imply? When exploring the many superstitions of older times, it is an interesting way that some things were done. Many things were quite different from modern times as to thinking and every day life. Sometimes a modern person has to take that step back in looking at the paranormal in historical locations from that viewpoint.

Photo By: Dan LaFave

    This story with the mirror superstition had some plausible substance to the fact that it quite possibly could be true. They said at the Myrtles Plantation that this mirror had something like that occur where it was not covered properly in history and that a smudge stain that appears to be behind the actual glass can never be cleaned properly. After it is cleaned, they say those dark spot smudges come back and also sometimes take the form possibly of a spirit manifestation or spectral image to some people upon looking at this mirror. Some people have reported that they sometimes can see a ghostly apparition of a woman descending the reflected staircase looking at them in the mirror at an angle upon viewing the mirror even though they cannot see the actual apparition upon looking at the main staircase. I found those encounters extremely interesting.

I then walked around the property gardens in front of the house getting as many pictures as I could of everything. I saw that I was not the only person taking pictures that day, there was a bus load of tourists that had stopped by and many flashes were going off in different areas of the Myrtles Plantation property which I believes sits on 10 acres now, with a pond, neat little bridge, and gazebo in the back area of the property. The main house has a really large garden to the front area of the property and this garden takes on a very mysterious and misty look to it late at night that I later found out. There are also very strange things that take place on this property both during the day and night.

Photo By: Dan LaFave

As I walked around this whole property, I carefully surveyed it with my eyes so that I knew exactly what everything looked like by day, because at night of course it gets very dark and easy to confuse shapes in the darkness at a distance. I familiarized myself with the property the best I could and had a good time walking around and looking at everything for the very first time. I tried to also imagine to myself what life must have been like on this very old plantation back in the 1700's when it was built. Was it a good life, or was it a hard life. That also was a life of much slavery in those days. As we all know, slavery was a big thing in the south during those days, especially in Louisiana. It was hard for me to imagine what it must have felt like to be a slave during those harsh times, sometimes chained up.

Photo By: Dan LaFave (Caretakers Cottage)

The gardens again were very beautiful and mysterious looking. The Spanish moss hung from the Myrtle and Oak trees in such a way that as evening crept in on me, the whole house and property started to take on a really creepy look to it. I was still wondering when exactly my first ghostly paranormal activity experience was going to occur. A person can only imagine the anticipation that I felt.

Photo By: Dan LaFave (Front Garden Area)

Photo By: Dan LaFave (Front Garden Pathway)

It definitely was creepy looking to me.

I found myself suddenly standing in the front garden area with my camera looking back at the main plantation house.

114

By this time, the other daily tourists had left as well as much of the main staff for the day. It dawned on me then as to the anticipation that I was feeling. I was starting to realize that I was there alone at night with a very small group of other people who were staying overnight.

Photo By: Dan LaFave

Could see and feel the history of that plantation house as the sun set behind me and the darkness crept in for the evening. Was I possibly brought to this place for much more by something? That was the thought at the time....

Photo By: Dan LaFave

I felt a sensation walking up on the front porch. What was it?

Photo By: Dan LaFave

Back in 2005, not sure if they do this anymore, the main tour manager Esther would after the official history and story tours ended go all throughout the main plantation house and lock up. She would make sure that no people were still hanging around in there except for the paying overnight guests. She was a very nice woman, and I had the pleasure of sitting down with her quite awhile alone and talking about many things earlier that day as to both history and the many ghostly paranormal stories at the Myrtles Plantation. I took many mental notes from that discussion.

I wish I had filmed those personal interviews and discussion when I sat down with Esther back then just to have, because I found her to be a very friendly and interesting woman full of knowledge and history. The Myrtles Plantation after my own in depth paranormal investigation visit in 2005 took place was later featured on many paranormal television shows including Ghost Hunters on the SyFy television network, Ghost Adventures on The Travel Channel network, and Ghost Lab on the Discovery Channel network.. I am sure there were other television shows and documentaries as well. Things really seemed to bloom as to people really noticing The Myrtles Plantation shortly after my visit there. When I saw all those paranormal shows after I was already there investigating in 2005, I found it very interesting and intriguing because I had actually been there first to conduct an in depth paranormal investigation and encounter things for myself. I was vacationing of course, but I also had very serious notions as to doing my own paranormal investigative research there.

The house and property had been on some paranormal topic shows before that time, but never quite as to full detail and paranormal investigations taking place to really confirm things. After my visit there in 2005, the Myrtles Plantation seemed to be featured on television a lot. I also saw that a lot more people later went to explore and investigate it for themselves including several paranormal teams after my visit in 2005. As I stood in the front yard with the sun setting, I could hear and see her going throughout the house checking on things and locking up. She then came outside at one point and we bid farewell to each other for the night. I told her that I would be careful and sure not to accidently damage anything while investigating.

Photo By: Dan LaFave

I had earlier that day asked Ester if okay for me to walk around inside the house doing my investigation that night. She said that was perfectly okay as long as I was careful. She also mentioned that they in those days had to lock up the main lower parlor area of the house because of all the antiques and old paintings in there that were worth money. She actually told me that in the past that they used to leave that open at night for the overnight guests to walk around and look at, but that some guests had actually cut off pieces of the drapes to take home with them for souvenirs and stuff.

When I heard that, I just shook my head. What the hell would get into people as to doing such things and destroying another person's property, especially beautiful historical things such as what are inside the Myrtles Plantation? She said that the paintings in there were very valuable and that people had in the past even messed with those. I perfectly understood what she was saying. I also was disappointed, because that was one of the main areas that I wanted to investigate in. She had told me in those days that due to insurance reasons she wanted to allow me, but that they could not due to that situation.

Not sure if they allow overnight people now to be able to walk into the main parlor area of the house at night. I did however have access to most of the house areas luckily for those 4 nights investigating except for that particular area which would have been their formal living room and dining room areas back in the 1700's. I could peer inside the windows as to taking pictures and observing though, which I did.

After Esther left and I could no longer see any other vehicles in the parking lot, it dawned on me that I was really alone now. There was a very small group of guests sitting on the outside patio meeting area behind the house talking. I sat down and we all talked about paranormal things. When they all found out that I was what people consider to be a professional ghost hunter from Texas, they were ecstatic. Some of them asked to investigate with me that night. I could not wait to get started as to exploring and investigating. I also had the strong feelings at times of being watched both inside and outside the main plantation house. This feeling can be felt many times by a person throughout either the day or the night. It was a feeling where a person constantly is turning around to look for something, but that something is never quite visible to the naked eye, only by surprise it seems.

Photo By: Dan LaFave

Think we must have sat there for a few hours talking. I was asked by the small group of guests there as to what things I had seen in my life as a professional ghost hunter up to that point in 2005. I started to tell them my very true and startling paranormal/supernatural experiences that I have had as an investigator/researcher. I told them how I got into this, and what I have found, and also the many personal clients I had helped over the years as to understanding the very true paranormal ghostly phenomenon that was sometimes occurring in their homes and businesses.

I told them that the paranormal world is very mysterious and that it sometimes can be quite extreme and scary for certain people. As I told them about some of my own stories, I could see their eyes get very big and some of the women began to get nervous. Was it that they suddenly realized that they were going to be staying overnight in the haunted plantation house behind us? Or was it that they suddenly realized that the paranormal ghostly world was much more real than what they had experienced personally in their own lives? I realized then that those people had never had a real ghostly paranormal experience. That was why they were there at the Myrtles Plantation that night.

Some of the women acted like they did not even want to go back inside the house to their rooms that night. Was it my stories or was it the feeling they were getting from the house at that moment? As we talked, I saw some people turning and looking at things on the back porch area. I asked them what they were looking at. They said that out of the corner of their eye, they saw what looked like children moving. At that moment, we all heard a loud noise by the back door to the main parlor area, the area where the main inside staircase is. This was a noise like someone had banged against it from inside.

We all got up to look, and examined the door.......but no one was there and no one as inside. As a matter of fact, we were told that no one that night was actually staying in that largest upstairs suite of the house. So, I knew there was not anyone up there. I looked up at one point to one of the upstairs windows of that suite, and could swear that I saw a dark shaped outline of a pacing person move past the window a few times as if they were looking back down at all of us sitting on that back patio area.

I was staying again in the other next largest downstairs suite which was directly beneath this other area of the house. As it got late with people heading to their rooms for the night, I headed to my room to check equipment and get ready for my first solo paranormal investigation run of the house and property that night. Some of those other people would join me later that night, but I never saw them.

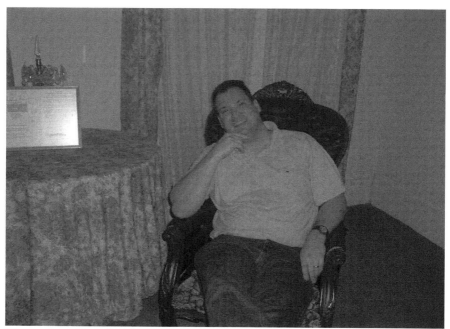

Photo By: Dan LaFave

I again could not wait to get fully started as to this first nightly investigation there. Thinking back, I do remember the anticipation I felt then which was very high.

In my room, I was taking pictures and documenting things as well as doing some poses for memory sake. I could feel things the whole time in there, that I definitely was not alone. I could also feel at times that I could hear unseen movement within the two rooms. One time I heard a loud knock as if the staff were at the door. When I went to see who it was, there was no one outside or around.

Photo By: Dan LaFave

I was very happy to be there and obviously smiling, but inside I was also wondering about things.......

Again, this great house from my memory was pretty big, even bigger it seems from first looking and reviewing. I remembered all the previous reading I again did in Frances Kermeen's book "The Myrtles Plantation". By this time, it was pretty dark outside. And when I say dark, it gets pretty dark on this old plantation at night because the trees block out whatever natural light there is. I found myself looking at that front garden area again with my digital audio recorder, video camcorder, and EMF detector in hand. If there was a way of carrying more items with me, I would have.

By that time, some people actually did come out and join me along with their digital cameras out in the garden. It was about 10 pm or so and again pretty dark out there except for the lights that were positioned throughout this garden. Our small group of 5 to 6 people was standing there looking around. Earlier in our discussion on the back patio, one of the women mentioned that she had heard a pretty credible story from several people who had stayed there about a ghost cat. Now when she mentioned this term ghost cat, I admit that I almost laughed until I heard more of that story from her. I had read up on and heard many ghostly stories about the Myrtles Plantation over the years, but never did I ever come across any accounts of a ghost cat. Everyone upon hearing her begin to tell this ghostly story all turned and listened.

Photo By: Dan LaFave

The story goes that there is a ghost cat that sometimes walks the property of the Myrtles Plantation at night. No one knows for sure how this cat came to become a ghost cat,

124

but it appears that it may have belonged to the long ago caretaker who actually was killed or committed suicide. This is where this story gets very strange as to the paranormal part of it.

Some people have had encounters where they are walking around the property investigating or looking for things just like us. This is when they spot this cat in the front area of the garden. People would say that this cat would walk towards them and then stop and then stare at them. Then it would into the bushes and disappear. Well, so far this story seemed very natural to me. Then she said that people would snap pictures of the garden area of this strange looking cat, and that the cat would not show up in any pictures that they took.......only the garden area behind the cat.

Now, my ears perked up upon hearing this and also the seriousness in her voice. We however earlier that evening upon hearing this said it was strange, but none of us had encountered that, so we assumed this story was just a myth or made up urban legend as people call them. While we were standing in front of the main house taking the pictures, I noticed a movement to our right. I turned and started looking. The other people noticed me doing this and looked too. We all saw a grey striped cat approaching us from the right side of the garden. This cat was a pretty good size also. The strange part is that this cat did not seem afraid of us, but at the same time it walked a very straight pattern of travel towards the sidewalk path that goes into the garden. We were all watching to see what this cat would do next.

When the cat got to the garden sidewalk path approximately 40 to 50 feet in front of our group, the cat stopped and sat down looking straight at us. Even though this seemed just like a solid ordinary prowling cat to me, I was feeling something different and I remembered that story she had told us earlier. I also looked over at that same woman standing to the side of me. I raised my digital camera carefully and slowly so not to startle this sitting cat, and I snapped a focused picture with flash of this cat. I then looked down at my camera to look at the picture. I could see that same garden area in front of me with the sidewalk, but no cat was showing on my camera. I gasped, "Oh God, look".

The group of people with about 4 to 5 digital cameras then all raised their cameras and starting shooting pictures of this cat. The flashes were just crazy, and any real cat was sure to have run upon all this activity and flashes taking place, but this cat sat its ground just looking at us. It also was a solid cat to the naked eye for us. When we all looked at our digital cameras, we all looked up with the same very surprised expressions on our faces. In all of those pictures, which must have been at least 20.......there was not one image of that cat showing up. The pictures were all clear as well with no distortions in them. All those pictures simply looked as if we were just taking pictures of the front garden area.

While we were looking at our pictures and making our comments of extreme surprise, we did not notice the cat walk off. When we looked up, this cat had vanished from sight and was no longer there. We walked over to that area and carefully looked throughout the garden shining our flashlights, but there was no cat to be seen. We had many puzzled questions at that point. What did we just see? Was this a spectral ghostly cat that we just witnessed? Was this just a trick of the eye and all of our cameras? The answer to that question is quite clear upon all our observations and opinions, we all were pretty sure that we had just seen the ghost cat.

I was blown away by that paranormal experience and could not wait to see and experience more at the Myrtles Plantation that night. The night was young for me even though those people were starting to wear down for the night. Some of them appeared really freaked out by what had just occurred to us. We disbanded and some people went back to their rooms for the night. It was around midnight by this time. I was just getting started in my paranormal investigative plans for the night. There was much more to come as to seeing and experiencing very strange things.

Photo By: Dan LaFave

I traveled to Louisiana and the Myrtles Plantation with a former female partner as to both a vacation and also as to me conducting my sole paranormal investigative research as to the many stories and accounts by people over the years. She also was never really into the paranormal world the way that I was and am now and spent much of her time in the room while I investigated the house and grounds. I later met and married my wife Connie through paranormal circles who is very much in this paranormal world with me now as to investigating and we have been happily together for 6 years now. I mention as to that other unnamed former female partner for one sole reason here, and that is to tell this next paranormal encounter experience.

I had gone back up to the room and managed to coax her to come out a little and hang out on the back patio. She sat down at one of the tables back there alone while smoking. It was pretty late and quiet by this time around 1:00 am or so. I told her that I was going to the back of the main house up on the back porch area to do some more investigative exploring and walked off with my same trust equipment. I took the path between the main house and office area to head back there. This is the same path area that is also shown in the famous ghostly apparition of the slave Chloe. I will also tell you about my own encounter with the ghostly apparition of Chloe later in this chapter.

While investigating on the back porch area, I stayed right in that same area being quiet and not moving around much. Not much was happening to me and I never heard any voices or anything. I also never strayed from that particular area. I picked up my equipment and went back the exact same direction and path that I took from the patio before between the office building and the main house. As I walked between the buildings, I could see the shocking look on the female partner's face as I walked out of the shadows towards her. She kept looking at me as if she had just seen a ghost. She also kept asking me several times if I was playing around trying to scare her. I looked at her very surprised and said no, that I was on the back porch the whole time very quietly. I asked her why she was looking at me strangely as I sat down.

Then she told me what had just happened to her. She said that she had turned and seen me walk between the buildings and disappear from sight. She said that she then just sat there calmly smoking her cigarette looking around. She then said that she heard a strange noise down the long lighted sidewalk that leads from the patio area alongside the back of the main house all the way to the parking lot. There are approximate two to three lamp posts that line this sidewalk as to lighting it at night and they come automatically on when it gets dark. When she was looking down this long sidewalk past the room and far end of the main house there as to that strange noise, she says that a very shadowy dark figure then started to walk around from that side of the house.

She could not see it very clearly because it was still pretty far away from her, but she said that it was a very tall male shape figure and it walked very stiff like and slowly in its steps as it rounded the corner and started to walk down that sidewalk towards her. She says that she got up to get a better look and then realized something as it got closer.......that it looked just like me. She stated that she yelled towards it thinking it was me and told me to stop fooling around with her. I use the word me for the sake of what I am leading up to here.

I am six foot five inches tall which is pretty tall for a man. There are not many men my height or taller. She said that as the figure got closer it then stopped and just stared at her. She said that the face was in the shadows where she could not see the expression, but she said that it was wearing the same clothes as me and looked exactly like me. She again told me to quit playing around with her. The problem is that it was not really me. She says that the figure stood there and then turned started to walk a little faster this time back down the sidewalk away from her going back the exact same way it had come before.

This is what led her to think that I was playing a practical joke trying to scare her really badly. The problem again here is that whatever she saw was not me at all because I was never on that side of the house and I did not do it to her. It took me several minutes of discussion to convince her that I had not played a joke or anything on her and that whatever she saw was definitely not me. I was just as surprised and blown away as she was. This led me to believe strongly that what she had witnessed was for all paranormal ghostly reasons, my doppelganger.

No one really knows what doppelgangers really are, but it is believed that they are a spiritual ghostly entity that takes the identical shape of a person or animal as in trying to get the attention of someone. No one knows again what they really are or why they sometimes appear to some people. I myself have never actually witnessed a doppelganger, but my wife Connie has. Believe or not, my wife Connie witnessed again my doppelganger shape/form standing in front of her during a past paranormal investigation we did. She says she also saw me and that it looked just like me from behind.

The only problem again is that I came up behind her at that moment really surprising her. When she looked back in front of her, she says that the doppelganger had disappeared. It all was very strange indeed. It seemed to me at the time that what the main sign read before "The Home Of Mystery and Intrigue" was very true.

Photo By: Dan LaFave

Much later that night after going to sleep, I suddenly could hear movement noises both above the room, in the adjoining sitting room, as well as the locked adjoining room to the front of the house. I tried to peer through the keyhole trying to see into that locked room, but could not see anything. But I heard it.......and it sounded like a person moving and at times I could hear voices as well. The main issue is that I knew for sure that no one was staying in the upstairs bedroom up above and that they had totally locked the main parlor area and that other room. There was no way someone could have been in those two rooms.

The next day, I moved over into the Fannie Williams room which is claimed to have been the old bedroom of the children. They also have this room decorated and set up looking as to this. The room has two doors. One coming in from one side hallway entrance and the other door to the main foyer house area is locked up tight where it cannot be opened for a reason. Many people have witnessed seeing the apparitions of the two children who were poisoned long ago in this room, other rooms, and outside on the property.

The ghostly children apparitions are sometimes even seen playing outside on the roof eave outside the upstairs people's windows. People have even captured pictures before of what looks to be ghostly children up on the roof and in the house besides seeing them with the naked eye. It is said that they communicate as well playing and trying to get people's attention. People during both tours and staying overnight in the rooms will claim they feel tugging on their clothing and tapping from behind and turn around and do not see anything.

This is also the same room that I was able to capture then one of my most amazing ghostly EVP's ever. This EVP to me is not just an EVP. I say this because I have captured many amazing and clear communicative EVP's during the time that I have been seriously researching the paranormal world from years ago. This particular EVP captured by my digital audio recorder stands out from the rest for one very important point......I managed to captured three different very distinctive clear and loud EVP ghostly voices all speaking at the same time after each other in a matter of a few seconds. I have this great EVP from years back on our YouTube channel "Seeking The Real Paranormal Truth...." for anyone to listen to.

What led to this EVP being obtained is even more interesting. Earlier that day, I had taken one of my digital audio recorders and put it on a table in the empty Fannie Williams room. I then hit record on the audio recorder and left the room locking the door as I left. I wanted to see what exactly the digital audio recorder would pick up when no one was in that room. I then went outside and eventually forgot about the recorder. I was out on the outside patio talking with some people that evening. It was not dark yet. A very young couple in their twenties did drive up to walk around and visit the Myrtles Plantation. They walked up to me and were asking me about the plantation, about what I had seen so far, and what it was like. They also asked what the rooms were like because they had never been there before. I decided to take them both up to my room for a minute to show them.

As I unlocked the door and we entered the room, I still did not remember the digital audio recorder and none of us saw it sitting on the far end table in the room. There was an old toy wooden chest in there with different toys. We had heard stories that if people took these toys and placed them on the floor; that the ghostly children would play with them and move them sometimes. So, we were busy doing all of this on the floor for a few minutes talking about some things before we left and I locked up the room again. We were only in there a few minutes, and I know for sure that no one noticed or touched that digital audio recorder.....at least no one still living who was in that room.

I was sitting out on the patio with some other people and remembered after they left about 20 minutes later about the audio recorder. I ran up to the room and could not wait to listen to it. It was then that I realized that it had been recording when I had brought that young couple into the room. For several minutes on that recorder, there was extreme silence and sounded very boring to me. I was starting to get very disappointed.

When I got to the point where I could hear myself opening the door and myself and them talking and doing things, I really was getting discouraged due to the noise. I thought to myself, I must not have gotten anything and now all I hear is us in the room talking about the toys, children, and paranormal things that happen in the room to people. There is this sometimes loud discussion between us of the history of the house and what must have taken place there before. There is also discussion and question as to if their ghosts still possibly exist in that house and on the property. This is when it happened and my eyes got really big upon hearing it for the first time.

Did I just capture on my digital audio recorder what I thought I was hearing? I rewound the audio recorder and listened to that part again. I could not believe what I was hearing very loud and clear over and over on that recorder as I played it. There were our voices of myself and the couple in the background, but here were three very clear, louder, scary sounding voices in a matter of a few seconds of each other on that recorder.

To this day, it makes me remember back and shiver. I could first hear someone or something moving the audio digital recorder even though I know for a fact that when we were in the room, no one was even close to it. Right after the movement recorder noise as woman, possibly the slave Chloe, yells "We Are Not Sleeping!" A few seconds after that ghostly EVP occurs another little innocent sounding girl's voice comes on and says "Help Me". A few seconds after that little girl's ghostly voice, a very scary and ominous much older man's voice with an accent comes on saying something in a full sentence as well, but not sure on the exact sentence. To me on a large speaker playing it, I thought that could hear the words 'pay the reaper' in the middle of his very loud expressive sentence of several words. All this time, I could also hear my own voice and the voices of that young couple in the background of the Fannie Williams room. This just sent chills down my spine when I heard it for the first time.

I traveled to the Grace Episcopal historic church and cemetery the next day. I had no idea it was even there till someone told me about it. When I got there, I could not believe how old this cemetery was. I saw cemetery markers and crypts with dates back to the 1700's on them. Walking around inside this cemetery taking pictures really took me back in history. This cemetery is rather large and when you are in the back really old area alone, you can feel things there. I even crawled inside an old crypt that was open with nothing inside it, and it also had a back door. This was very creepy to me. Someone told me that they sometimes removed the remains over time to replace with someone else as history went on.

Photo By: Dan LaFave

I just loved taking pictures in there.

Photo By: Dan LaFave

Evening quickly came and I started to get a really eerie feeling in that cemetery. Almost as if the past was going to reach out and grab me. I walked around till it became too dark to see, and then headed back to the parked vehicle to head on back to the Myrtles Plantation for that night's investigation to begin.

When I started this investigation around 12 pm that night, I headed over to the back of the house up on the porch. I was looking into the main area trying to see what things were going on in there, both by filming with the camcorder and by taking pictures. I could feel something in there staring back out. I just could not put my finger exactly on what I was feeling. This night was particular spooky to me as a paranormal investigator.

While peering through the window, I suddenly heard movement inside the main parlor locked off area. I put my head closer to try and get a better look through the darkness. I could make out shapes through the darkness pretty well as to the antique furniture and other things inside. I then heard the noise again. What was it? What was I hearing? It sounded to me like someone walking around in there and it was not coming from upstairs where the guests stay in the rooms on the second floor. I put my face right up against the window glass to see.

At that moment, I heard a very loud shuffle on the wooden floor inside and definitely knew at that moment that I was not imagining this. I said in a clear loud rational voice out loud, "I know you are in there, I can hear you, quit hiding and show me!" I soon realized that was the wrong choice of words to use in that situation. I suddenly heard five to six very loud boot sounding thudding footsteps coming at the window from the other side in that main parlor room. Then something that I can only describe as an invisible hand smacked the glass really hard from the other side right where my face was. It smacked the glass that the whole window vibrated very loudly.

This really startled and made me jump. When this happened, I went back really fast through uncontrolled surprise motion. This event really made me go back fast through normal body impulse. I took four steps back really fast in total shock and fear, and nearly fell off that high porch which stands at least six feet off the ground in the back where the air conditioner main units are. I almost went backwards off that porch falling onto those air conditioners. I could have really injured myself upon falling, but I managed to grab something and stop my fall. I then just stood there staring back at that dark window which went from the ceiling all the way to the floor.

Back in history, they used to open these windows in such a way that a person about five and half feet could walk right through. The windows all around the house were like this, where they also open to help ventilate the house against the very tough thick Louisiana heat and humidity. I was also told that back in history, they used to hold grand affairs and dancing in plantation homes like this, where they sometimes would dance inside and outside of all these opened up large windows that were like doorways. In the main parlor area where they greeted their guests, there were also separate men and women meeting social areas of the house. The women's meeting area of the Myrtles Plantation house was on the left side while the men's area was on the far right side. Apparently, when it came to important meeting affair discussions in those days, the men made those decisions in private in their own meeting area.

One of the main ghostly stories and legends of the Myrtles Plantation involves Chloe, who was a main female house slave and servant. It appears that she had special privileges from the other owned slaves by the owner of the house Judge Clarke Woodruff and it is also said that she quite possibly also was his mistress. Because of this special arrangement, she lived in and was allowed to do many things within the house for the family and in caring for their children.

It is said that one day Chloe was eavesdropping on Judge Woodruff and other men as they were having a meeting and discussing things in the closed door men's area of the house. She had put her ear up to the door as to trying to listen to what was said. It appears that she had done this before as well in trying to gain more power and status as to her position within the house. This day, however, Judge Woodruff caught her listening again and had previously warned her of this kind of thing. As punishment for her action, it is said that he cut off her left ear and banished her back to the slave area settlement on the very large plantation at the time that was down by the Mississippi River. Chloe wore a head scarf wrapped totally around her head to hide her disfigured left ear. I was told that this plantation was very large as to those days in history, that the land property covered much of what St. Francisville is today and more. Over time, much of the property was sold as to the present size of the plantation property as it stands and appears today.

The story and legend goes that Chloe then devised a plan as to trying to get back into good status with Judge Woodruff and his family……and get back into the main house. It is said that she missed caring for the children a lot. It is said that one day, one of the Judge's young daughters (around nine years old) was having a birthday party celebration. Chloe volunteered and made a strong point to make the birthday cake for that celebration. Her plan was to crush Oleander (a toxic poisonous plant) leaves and mix a few of those poisonous crushed leaves into the cake. Her plan towards grace was to try to make the children sick and then nurse them back to health in her hopes of getting back to good grace with Judge Woodruff.

It appears that Judge Woodruff was away that day for the birthday party on business matters. Mrs. Woodruff and the children ate that birthday cake only to become very ill from it. Chloe had misjudged the dosage of the poisonous crushed leaves she had put into the cake. She had only put a very small amount of it into the cake, but that dosage was enough to be fatal and it is said that Mrs. Woodruff and the two children died from it very suddenly. Judge Woodruff returned soon to find himself a widower, and soon questioned as to how this occurred.

When Chloe found out how sick Mrs. Woodruff and the two children were, she had possibly made comments to the rest of the slaves about what she had done. They told Judge

Woodruff. The story and legend then goes that the slave Chloe was hung by a tree down on the property. From this much told story and legend, this is why many people believe that the ghosts and spirits of Chloe, the two children, Mrs. Woodruff, and even Judge Woodruff still linger and haunt the Myrtles Plantation to this day. Many people including myself have witnessed their ghostly apparitions in that house and on the property.

On the last night into my paranormal investigation at the Myrtles Plantation, I again thought of the many stories and encounters by people that I had heard. There was a story in the main front entrance stairway area, that a person can sometimes hear footsteps dragging and ascending the stairs as if a person was struggling to get to the top. It is said that William Winter, also a past owner of this house, was outside one day and was shot. That he staggered back into the house calling for his wife and that he either walked or crawled up the stairs to the 17th step where he collapsed dying in his wife's arms. People told me that they had heard those loud footsteps at times late into the night ascending those main stairs from the doorway.

That final night I was staying in the main largest Judge Clarke Woodruff suite upstairs in that main part of the plantation house. As I set up my paranormal equipment in the main foyer area really close to the piano in there, I started to hear things. It was really dark and I did not have my flashlight on or my video camcorder going yet. I did not even have my digital audio recorders on or recording yet. As I was crouching doing the setup in the dark of my camcorder on a tripod, I heard a movement noise in the darkness behind me. I did not know what it was and kept turning around to see nothing there. I then felt a tug on the back of my shirt that really got my attention. Something unseen had grabbed my shirt from behind.

I could feel the temperature dropping very suddenly at that point as I stood there in the darkness looking around. What the hell had just grabbed me? I had felt a small hand doing that. At that moment I heard a noise coming from behind the locked door to my right that I was told was the women's old meeting area room that I previously talked about. I could not get into either that room or the main parlor area, even though I could look through the glass locked door leading into the parlor.

This area to the left of the stairs was where I was going to put my camcorder recording looking into that parlor as I investigated. After a few minutes of standing there looking around in the darkness, I turned back around to attend to my camera stuff. It was then that I heard it. Something that again made me jump. Someone called my name 'Dan' out of that darkness behind me. It was the sound of a child. I also clearly heard my name. Something or someone was trying to get my attention. I looked around again for several minutes shocked but could find nothing, and I again unfortunately did not have my digital audio recorder on and recording yet at the time I heard this. That would have been one hell of a good paranormal audible voice evidence capture if I those recorders would have been on.

Nothing else out of the ordinary occurred to me while I investigated down there for at least two hours. After awhile, I did not feel strange anymore and was getting tired. I knew the next day that I also had to drive that long distance back to Texas. I packed up everything and headed for the room upstairs and went to sleep. Before I went to sleep, I put all of my packed up paranormal equipment at the far side of the large Judge Clarke Woodruff suite. There was also a bright moon out that night that shown through the windows up there. I soon fell deep asleep.

Later that night, I was awoken by a loud movement noise in the room. I remember opening my eyes lying there on the bed. I turned my head to look around the darkness of the large room. I panned right and then left of the room as my eyes focused. It was then that I saw it. Standing over across the room from me by the fireplace, was the dark shape figure of what looked like a woman. I knew this because the moonlight was shining through the window behind her outlining her shape pretty good. She was also solid looking. I then saw this as well.......she had a headband scarf wrapped around her head. She was just standing there approximately 10 to 15 feet away just staring at me. I did not feel a feeling of fear or anything. I could not see her face, but her clothing looked like the clothing from far back in history.

My first thought at that moment was to try to get a picture. But all my paranormal equipment was across the room. There was no way this ghostly spirit was going to stay there long enough for me to do that. I just lay very still as to my body and just had my head turned a little bit as to looking at her. This all just lasted approximately 45 seconds, because I then adjusted my body a little trying to get a better look, and the ghostly apparition in front of me just vanished into the darkness. She had not moved; it just vaporized in front of my eyes as I blinked.

I then questioned rationally as to what I had just witnessed. I also again remembered all my ghostly paranormal experiences that I had over that whole 4 day and night paranormal investigation. As I went over everything in my head, I knew that what I witnessed as to hearing and seeing things was very real. I had not imagined any of this because I have always been a very well balanced paranormal investigator/researcher with a certain degree of skepticism and logic as to paranormal encounters or any evidence acquired.

Over those 4 days and nights at the Myrtles Plantation in St. Francisville, Louisiana, I had witnessed and experienced many very strange unexplainable paranormal and supernatural things. These events in my opinion were also very extreme for any investigator. In looking at and reviewing all those stories/encounters by other people and also from what I had personally experienced and witnessed back in 2005, I could clearly see that the historic Myrtles Plantation was indeed very haunted.

Photo By: Dan LaFave

Chapter 7: La Borde House
(Rio Grande City, Texas)

Photo By: Dan LaFave

Earlier in 2012, myself, my wife Connie, and our team Graveyard Shift Paranormal Investigations with present members consisting then of Javier (Harvey) Martinez, Jerry Alexander, and also a very new investigator in training on her very first investigation with us had the pleasure of investigating the historic La Borde House in Rio Grande City, Texas. We were also joined by other experienced paranormal investigators Jay Villarreal out of San Antonio, Texas and Alejandro Dominguez (The Dead Explorer) out of Austin, Texas for this special filmed investigation documentary project which is shown on the internet. This was not just any ordinary every day paranormal investigation, not that any of our investigations are ordinary because most of what we do is exciting.

This again was a special investigation. I had specifically and personally set up with management of La Borde House for us to have complete access as to a very in depth paranormal investigation to confirm to ourselves if the many stories of ghostly haunting activity were true or not. Again, I and our team had done extensive research before even going in to investigate this now historic Texas hotel which was a former family home back in the day. We also set up for a local news station reporting crew Telemundo 40 out of McAllen, Texas to personally join us that night for the investigation so they could experience along with us what it was like.

We all also were going to stay overnight in the hotel after our investigation totally free of charge as to the great courtesy and hospitality of the hotel management. I, my wife, and the other present members of our team were very appreciative of that and we all looked forward to it. We were also joined by two other paranormal investigators out of San Antonio and Austin for this exciting paranormal investigation which was aired live by Telemundo 40 on October 31 (Halloween night) and November 1, 2012 by Telemundo 40 in two special paranormal investigation broadcasts that can be seen on the internet and also our paranormal YouTube channel.

Photo By: Dan LaFave

This was a paranormal night that we were not to ever forget because of what happened to us. Many paranormal investigators and researchers just don't experience things like what occurred that night and we had a news reporting crew there with us to experience things with us and tell the story of La Borde House and its many ghostly haunting stories. La Borde House has also been investigated by the SyFy television network show Ghost Hunters years before.

143

They did not find a whole lot during that investigation, and the paranormal encounters there were mixed over time that I personally researched. Some people found extreme things, while other people found nothing.

Photo By: Dan LaFave (Our Documentary Video)

After talking with both present and former staff members, walking around and touring the hotel, and hearing some more stories and paranormal encounters by people, we got all our paranormal gear out of the vehicles unpacked and set up for the investigation. We also obtained video interviews to be included in our video documentary which again is on YouTube called 'The Ghosts Of La Borde House'.

There are the ghostly haunting stories of the woman in red seen throughout the property at times and also in The Red Room. She appears sad and to be looking for something. The story says that she quite possibly could be the long lost daughter of the former owner and that upon her father finding out that she was a prostitute, she threw herself off the front balcony to her death on the pavement below. There is an actual etching of her name in the brick on the patio very near the door of The Red Room and people think she sketched this into the brick. No one can erase it either, they have tried. The name keeps coming back.

This corner upstairs room is decorated entirely in red and is very beautiful and elegant looking. There are also other ghostly apparitions seen sometimes as to children playing, and a man. They said that they believe and think possibly of the male spirit to be of the former original owner Mr. La Borde himself. Francois La Borde had this beautiful, historic, and very large home actually designed by French architects in Paris in 1893, and the home was later built and finished in 1899. Walking around the home, a person can see the French architecture which looks a lot like homes throughout New Orleans, Louisiana. There are areas in deep South Texas region where the French influence as to architecture was very evident.

Walking around this house and property, myself, my wife Connie, and the rest of our team were really impressed by how they have restored this old home. This was a historic hotel that I and my wife would just simply enjoy staying in at times due to its charm. The hotel staff is so friendly also and will easily tell you their stories and ghostly encounters that they have had or heard about from other guests.

We had dinner and then set up all our paranormal equipment for that night's very in depth paranormal investigation. We waited for the Telemundo 40 news reporting crew to get there. When they arrived, they initially did interviews with us talking about the history of the hotel that we knew about and also the ghostly stories we had heard about. Then they joined us while we investigated the La Borde House.

There is something very unique about this hotel that is different than many historical locations we have investigated before. This hotel has a sealed up underground tunnel under it. This is not a basement or anything. It actually was a tunnel built it is believed in prohibition days connecting to the border with Mexico. It is believed that both alcohol and illegal immigrants were brought through this underground cement walled tunnel long ago. When a person visits the hotel, they can venture down into this tunnel which is pretty spooky.

When we went down there by ourselves and also with the new reporting crew to do an EVP recording session, we were spooked by a bat that was flying around our heads down there. This was pretty funny. We did, however, hear very strange ghostly things down there and had the strong sensation of being watched. It also got very cold down there for unexplainable reasons and one of our investigators, Jay Villarreal, felt like he was touched on the leg. As we came back up out of the tunnel, he advised me that he felt like he was touched by something and his leg in that area was now becoming hot.

As we got back up to the main control station room where we had our camera DVR system and rest of equipment set up, we started reviewing some things. We were also talking about that experience and things heard in the tunnel when Jay yelled frantically for us to come look. He was standing in the corner with his pants leg up on that leg. He then put his leg up on a chair. Right in front of all our eyes, three to four very distinctive and swelling long red scratch marks were forming and very clear on his leg. They looked to be bleeding slightly. Like claws or someone with very long finger nails had swiped at him.

We immediately got out video camcorder filming on this and several pictures were taken at the time. We captured the total progression of these scratches forming right in front of all of our eyes. He had undoubtedly been scratched by some unseen ghostly paranormal force. This is all seen on our video that we did which again is on YouTube to watch. We had a very hard time believing what had just occurred, but it all as right there in front of our eyes as it happened. We did not believe this was demonic or anything because there have to be a lot more signs as to something like that. But, whatever did this to his leg was very aggressive as to a ghostly spirit entity.

We all as a team split off throughout the night along with the news reporting crew as we investigated the hotel. We ran several EVP recording sessions and did other experiments like ITC with the P-SB7 Spirit Box and other things. On that Spirit Box, we picked up several what sounded like unnatural ghostly voices in direct response to our questions. There were also answers in Spanish coming through.

These experimental investigating sessions were done in both the room (Audobon Room) where it is said and reported that the past owner committed suicide in hanging himself while in great emotional distress from the roof rafter and also the Red Room where it is said that the female apparition is seen. We also did it in the room where it is said the ghostly children are either heard or seen playing at times at night by guests. The news reporting crew was there getting everything on camera as well and they were very nervous and very wide-eyed as things happened. Their big video started malfunctioning during those moments, and the actual cameraman had things grabbed out of his hand by some mysterious invisible force. They were genuinely freaked out by the paranormal events occurring.

This hotel is very large and has a very authentic Texas western feel to it. This hotel features rooms having very unique names......there again is The Red Room, The Audobon Room, The Rio Grande Room, The Ringgold Room, The Maria Tejas Room, and The Texian Room. We had several cameras set up that night and we were observing very closely from our base station DVR camera system set up downstairs in the other large eloquent historic looking La Borde Room. There is a large formal room downstairs across from the main office with many older pictures and furniture to look at. A person can stay overnight for a very reasonable price in any of these rooms......if they think they can handle it.

As the night carried on, we were all from time to time experiencing very strange things which did not appear naturally caused. That is, we were not able to debunk anything upon careful examining events as they occurred. Everything to us was startling and genuinely paranormal. At one point, we were recording up in the Red Room with three digital audio recorders going as well as filming. It was I, Jay Villarreal, and Alejandro Dominguez. Everyone else was downstairs. We had asked questions and upon playback, we heard a ghostly little girl say very clearly and loudly "Mama". She sounded to be only about 5 to 6 years old, maybe younger.

This really shocked us because there were movement noises near the bathroom when we obtained this Class A EVP on that digital audio recorder. The other very strange part is that only one audio digital recorder picked that very clear EVP up, there was nothing heard on the other ones. And we were all three standing and filming in a tight circle when obtained. We also obtained other very strange EVP's that were heard at that moment. We were recording only a few minutes at a time asking questions, and then played back immediately while filming everything to see what we would hear on the recorders. We did this for about 20 minutes.

Upon going back downstairs and telling everyone, we were in the base station control room playing the EVP recordings and talking about it. Everyone was inside the La Borde Room. My wife Connie always does something special during our investigations and this is when some of our most spectacular clear and loud EVP's have been captured over time. She always takes her recorder, even when we are taking a break, and puts the recorder on record mode and sits it on the base station.

My wife Connie did it the same way again as always and it was the only digital audio recorder going and we had even turned off the video camcorders then to recharge during our break. We were talking pretty loudly, and that is when we all heard it at the same time. A very loud and clear voice came from outside that room from the top of the stairs. The problem was that there was for sure no one up there. It was the very clear and audible voice sound to the ears as to a little girl shouting what sounded to us like "Coming Down" and it came right from the top area of the stairs.

We all at the same time stopped talking immediately and turned in complete shock towards the outside hallway. We then filed into the hallway very quickly as we could and all looked upstairs. There was no one around at all that we could find as to what created that little girl's very loud voice. The scary thing to myself and the rest of the paranormal group is that the loud audible voice we just heard was the exact sound of the ghostly little girl's voice we had captured on the recorder upstairs saying "Mama".

Our whole paranormal investigative crew was just astonished by this event that had just occurred. Did we all just hear at the exact same moment that audible and loud voice? What was it? Questions were asked out loud then. There were also exclamations yelled out loud for several minutes of this paranormal event happening. We had a static cam set at the top of the stairs but it did not capture any strange figure standing or moving there in that area. There was no one moving about upstairs on all of our static surveillance cams set up there at many angles. There were some strange light anomalies seen upstairs on the cameras a few minutes before, but we do not know if that was from headlights as to a vehicle on the main street outside. Our static cameras unfortunately did not have any audio connection as to picking up that voice. Our paranormal investigative group determined that this little girl's ghostly spirit was indeed playing around with us. Or so it appeared.

Our investigative group encountered quite a lot that night in the La Borde House. I looked at the news reporting cameraman sitting on an antique chair in the hallway. He was still nervously looking at his filmed footage. Everyone could see that both he and the news reporter from the Telemundo 40 local news station knew they had encountered something very strange and unnatural as to the ghostly paranormal along with us that night. Throughout the night, everyone had encountered cold spots and heard strange things. At one time, I was in the control room and I heard very loud boots walking across the floor up right above. These I could tell were heavy boots. I thought it was one of the investigators in that room, but I had not seen anyone go back upstairs. I went upstairs really quickly and walked into that room. There was no one in there.

Our group also had fun exploring and discovering things in the very interesting historic Texas home. Rio Grande

City, Texas is also a very interesting town. It is very near the United States and Mexico border. The Rio Grande River is very close by. I thought about that old concrete tunnel under the house and where it must lead to. It is sealed off, so a person wonders what actually sits behind that sealed off portion. Jay Villarreal told me that there must be a vast subterranean world of that tunnel and other connecting tunnels under Rio Grande City. People may never really know if true or just legend. We do know that underground tunnel is real.

After reviewing all the paranormal evidence and reviewing things again, we determined that the group had captured pretty amazing paranormal evidence and people in the group had extraordinary paranormal experiences. We also stayed the night, and myself and my wife stayed in the Red Room. We went to the room wondering what might happen to us that night while we slept, but we felt comfortable in that room. No one in the group saw any ghostly apparitions that night, but that does not mean they were not there. We did capture some amazing ghostly EVP's however. People in the group also had very strong feelings as to being watched and being touched. Jay Villarreal also had the event occur with the deep red swollen scratches appearing in front of all of our eyes. Alejandro Dominguez and Harvey Martinez in our group also had great experiences and encounters. My wife Connie was very perplexed by what occurred to us, and she along with me loved the beauty and history of the place.

All of the paranormal events our paranormal investigative group encountered there at La Borde House were amazing to us. We still had many questions as to why and how the ghostly paranormal things were happening and were wondering if the connections between the deaths of the people in history and the paranormal activity were connected. Our reasoning, perspectives, and intuition told us that there was a connection there. That somehow the ghostly paranormal world and history were quite possibly mixing at La Borde House. Did we think that La Borde House was haunted? Yes, in our opinion, along with other great paranormal data collected continuously by other people and based on the amazing paranormal evidence we collected, do believe it is haunted from our personal perspective. Our overall final analysis in the end supports this conclusion.

Photo By: Dan LaFave

Chapter 8: Stillman House (Brownsville, Texas)

Photo By: Dan LaFave

When Texas history and the ghostly paranormal world is deeply thought about seriously, the Stillman House in my personal opinion and others ranks up there with other good Texas historical locations as to paranormal activity. There are many stories by both regular every day people and paranormal investigators who have been there before. Is it possibly haunted? Let me tell you what we have witnessed and you can decide for yourself. Not too many people know about the Stillman House or the great paranormal activity that sometimes goes on in there both during the day or the night.

People sometimes while walking alone during the day touring the Stillman House or grounds encounter very strange things. I have spoken to very rational logical people who have had those ghostly encounters. I actually have had the opportunity as to investigating this very grand historic home along with our team group Graveyard Shift Paranormal Investigations a few times as to an in depth investigation into the night. Our investigative group has investigated the Stillman House with great evidence and results that were found. The Stillman House is run and maintained by the Brownsville Historical Association (BHA). I and my wife Connie also are members of this very good historical association as to helping to contribute in what ways we can for the historical preservation and other things in Brownsville, Texas.

Brownsville, Texas is a unique historic city with different locations of significance like the Stillman House, Fort Brown (where the university/college is located), Brownsville Heritage Museum, Alonzo Building, and Old City Cemetery. We have also investigated the Old City Jail building. This Texas city also sits on the border with Mexico in far South Texas. These locations all have a lot of history to them, some of it brutal as in the western conditions in Texas way back in those days. Again, people had a much rougher lifestyle back then, and some people died brutally and unjustly in the 1800's and early 1900's by the hands of others. This was the way of life in Texas and the old west. Life in long ago Texas frontier involved dying either by disease, the gun, the knife, or by hanging. Were there innocent people killed like this? Yes, there were in Brownsville and all across Texas.

As to moving to the Rio Grande Valley from San Antonio, Texas as an experienced paranormal investigator/researcher in 2008 and forming Graveyard Shift Paranormal Investigations, my wife Connie and I had no idea how much paranormal activity there was all throughout the who Texas Rio Grande Valley region. There was so much very interesting history to learn and acquire, and I enjoyed reading and researching on as much of this area's history that I personally could. We discovered and learned along the way as to exactly how much very active paranormal activity there was located right in Brownsville, Texas.......which is a lot. Could it again be Texas history mixing with the paranormal? That possibility definitely exists.

Upon investigating the historic Stillman House built by Henry Miller in 1850 and then rented to Charles Stillman and his family, we did not really have an idea as to what paranormal activity there was both in the house and the Brownsville Heritage Museum which is to the right of the house and part of the same museum historical complex. I saw that Charles Stillman while living in the house did many things as to helping Brownsville, Texas grow to what it is today. There over the years were exchanges as to ownership of the house as to information that can be found upon touring the house. The Stillman House is located at 1325 E. Washington Street.

A person can walk through the Brownsville Heritage Museum and read up on a lot about things from Brownsville, Texas past. There are many good books in the museum. The self-guided tour will show you a lot as well. Just look up the Brownsville Historical Association website for more information on everything. A lot of research can be found both in the museum, archives, and the great historical books and other things inside their gift shop. It is a very good museum as to the exhibits. We met Rhiannon Cizon, program and education coordinator for the museum, a few years ago and she does a lot of things there in her position as to setting up events, exhibits, and helping to run the museum.

If you need to know something good about any Brownsville history, just speak with either Rhiannon Cizon or Javier Garcia for either historical or paranormal information. They will be happy to tell you. They also have both historical and paranormal tours throughout the year and that information is posted on their website. If they do not know the information at that moment as to your question, they will try their best to find and personally answer it.

Our very first paranormal investigation inside the Stillman House was very interesting. When turning off the lights and starting a paranormal investigation, this house becomes pretty spooky inside and on the grounds. Even with the city streets right there, a person feels like they have stepped back into history.

Photo By: Dan LaFave

History in a lot of ways is what the paranormal is all about, because history sometimes can help to answer some possible paranormal activity questions. Or history can also help to confirm if the paranormal activity is indeed real. This can be accomplished by things such as acquiring ghostly EVP's on our recorders that answer specific questions as to either events or names in history having to do with the actual location. For example, if a paranormal investigator asks for someone to answer and a ghostly EVP is then possibly obtained with a voice stating a name like 'Charles Stillman', then that would be a direct link to the history of the house. There are also many other ways that we use as to our investigations.

Photo By: Dan LaFave

During our very first paranormal investigation, our team Graveyard Shift Paranormal Investigations/GSPI was not sure what exactly we would find within the Stillman House. Again, stories and encounters by other people are just that......stories and encounters till personally observed and witnessed. One woman had reported to me with a very shocked look that she had been at the Stillman House one day for an important daily meeting in the back meeting area of the Brownsville Heritage Museum. She had been outside talking on her cell phone right in front of the Stillman House. She had glanced at the house because she saw movement in one of the front windows which is the bedroom.

In her very shocked statement, she said that she all of a sudden saw another woman staring back at her from inside the Stillman House. Then the woman in the window vanished from sight. This woman also looked to be wearing much older clothing than modern times. The only problem with this whole story and encounter is that there were no people inside the Stillman House at the time. She had seen a ghost. Her eyes and expression showed that experience also.

When our paranormal research team investigated that first time, it seemed quiet. We did not really hear all too much and we did not see anything strange. We had heard movement noises at times during that investigation, but were not totally sure if what we heard was paranormal or not. We spent many hours in the house that night doing the investigation and went home pretty sleepy while the sun came up.

While reviewing our digital audio recorders, it was later discovered that the night was not quiet at all while we were investigating. Our team had acquired some very clear and amazing ghostly EVP's saying things to us. Some EVP's were in direct response to the investigator's questions. We were blown away and could not wait to go back and investigate the Stillman House again. These Class A EVP's are available to hear on the BHA's website and also on YouTube.

Photo By: Dan LaFave

Our team group also did public investigation events to raise money that was sponsored by us and the BHA around

Halloween. We did these public paranormal investigations with people paying to have the experience of seeing the paranormal side of the Stillman House for themselves while investigating alongside us. We also taught people from our experience over the years as to the right ways as to investigating the paranormal. We did these public events for both adults and also older teenagers. The female older teenagers we had with us in 2012 were just amazed by what happened and what they experienced with us.

During this paranormal investigation, our team used paranormal equipment which includes the experimental Ovilus X and K2 meter. Usually the Ovilus X that we have says only one to two word phrases that sometimes do not make any sense; sometimes they make sense in response. It is believed by paranormal researchers that this device can sometimes allow ghosts or spirits to communicate back to us through phonetic audio response because the device sense the field around it. For our investigation that night in the Stillman House, our Ovilus X as saying full sentences of several words in direct response sometimes to our questions. We were pretty sure that something ghostly from the paranormal world was trying to communicate with us as to that device.

One of the people joining us that night was also touched on her leg by what she described as an invisible hand. We asked out loud at that moment if the spirit touched her leg and the Ovilus X then said right after our question very clearly the words 'host' and 'once'. That was pretty scary to both us and her. She is okay though and has had no problems with the paranormal affecting her. All the people who joined us that night for the investigation really enjoyed themselves as to new paranormal discovery.

All of this evidence that was acquired is again available to watch and listen to on the Brownsville Historical Association's website and also on our YouTube channel "Seeking The Real Paranormal Truth......." with lots of great confirmed evidence captured by our investigate group. One thing that our investigative group does and always has done is analyze and carefully look at any possible paranormal evidence before we confirm and show that evidence to the public in any fashion.

As to investigating the history and the paranormal ghostly side of the Stillman House and Brownsville, Texas we found the paranormal activity very strong inside the house and on the property. There is even paranormal activity reported at times within the Brownsville Heritage Museum right next door. People while touring the museum have reported very strange things as well as museum staff members. I even worked for the BHA for a few months part-time once because I just love looking at history. There were times when I was either alone or with someone, and strange things were encountered both in the museum and inside the Stillman House. I always had a strange feeling any time I closed up for the evening and went into the house to turn off the lights and lock up.

The question remains as to whether we believe the Stillman House to be possibly haunted based on the amount of paranormal activity evidence found and discovered there. We asked that question before we investigated this historic house for ourselves to witness and experience things from a personal supernatural perspective. In looking at everything, we do believe that the paranormal activity is strong and constant enough at times to say that yes........the Stillman House is definitely a good historic Texas location to have a very haunted experience in. Just tell either Rhiannon, Javier, Priscilla, or any of the Heritage Museum staff members when you visit that Graveyard Shift Paranormal Investigations recommended this great historic house and museum for both great history and the paranormal.

Chapter 9: Fort Ringgold
(Rio Grande City, Texas)

Photo By: Dan LaFave

Early in 2012, myself, my wife Connie, and our investigative research group had the opportunity to investigate the historic Fort Ringgold located in Rio Grande City, Texas. This whole historic Texas fort sits on many acres and is very large with many historical converted fort buildings on it. This property is also watched and maintained by security staff and is owned and occupied by the Rio Grande City Consolidated Independent School District. Our investigative group acquired very special permission and authorization as to being able to investigate the whole property at night to see if the reported ghostly paranormal activity stories were true or not. People and also security staff at night experienced very strange things happening on the grounds of this old Texas fort.

This in my personal opinion is a very interesting historic Texas fort. Many people do not even know too much about this Texas fort or who commanded here back in the mid 1800's. Back in those days, this Texas fort was a very rugged Texas frontier and there again were many problems with Mexico which is right across the border and the Rio Grande River from this fort. Have you ever heard of The

Civil War? Who commanded the south during The Civil War?

General Robert E. Lee actually commanded Fort Ringgold in Rio Grande City, Texas a few years before The Civil War began. He was a colonel while at the fort before being promoted later when he withdrew from the fort command and took control and command of the Confederate Army. He had been sent to Fort Ringgold on a special mission out of Washington to deal with the Juan Cortina's War and the conflict that was taking place. He was sent to control the conflict.

Juan Cortina was considered a bandit by the United States. Our investigative group was joined by our friend and associate paranormal investigator Jay Villarreal for this special investigation. Jay is from Rio Grande City, Texas and knows a lot about the city and the fort's history. There is a historic restored house on the Texas fort property called the General Robert E. Lee house. Bet you did not know this little bit of very interesting information. The state of Texas actually does have some very interesting facts as to history and very important people who were here. If a younger person takes the time to look at both history and the paranormal, they will see that they both are very fascinating. History is anything but boring.......especially in Texas.

Everyone in our group unpacked all of their equipment upon arriving at Fort Ringgold and we set up our main DVR surveillance camera system inside the old hospital building of the fort, which now houses some administrative school district offices on the lower level. This is a pretty large building and this Texas fort complex again covered many acres and is very large. It took our group awhile of walking during the day just to tour and look at everything before we began the night's paranormal investigation.

Needless to say, we were tired that afternoon from all the walking, but it was very worth the experiences we had both from a historical and paranormal perspective. We also thanked the school district as to officially allowing our investigative paranormal team group Graveyard Shift Paranormal Investigations the awesome opportunity as to being able to investigate and explore this whole old fort complex that night. We loved the history of this location as well as what we found there paranormal wise.

The investigation actually started off a little slow without us really encountering things. I was beginning to wonder if anything would happen. We started the investigation around 7 to 8 pm that evening after setup of all the equipment. We also split up into 3 groups at times to investigate this large place with many buildings that we had complete access to. As the night continued, paranormal strange things began to pop up.

One of our investigative groups went down by the old warehouses on the fort property. This was a ways off from where we were set up as to the base station in the hospital. This group consisted of Javier (Harvey) Martinez, Jay Villarreal, and Romulo Cortez. They all started seeing very strange lights appearing and shining at them from inside the very dark old buildings there. They described it as happening quite a few times quickly in different locations as if people were shining flashlights at them from inside the buildings.

The main problem again with the scenario again was that there were no other people out there with us that night because they chased after the lights that seemed to move very quickly. There were no sounds of people running inside the buildings and all the buildings were very dark inside, there was no way any person could have been running around in those very dark buildings like that without injuring themselves or making a noise in trying to elude our investigators/researchers. Our investigators were also hearing very strange noises the same time these strange glowing lights appeared and disappeared many times in different building locations. Some of these buildings it is said were also the old horse stables from long ago for the soldiers.

My wife Connie and Jerry Alexander stayed behind as to monitoring things inside the old hospital on our DVR surveillance system. I headed out at one point to find the other group and came upon them calling out to the darkness and searching for those strange lights. I saw the very surprised looks on their faces. As I walked up from the darkness upon them, I also startled them because they were so busy looking for those strange lights, that they did not immediately know it was me approaching from the darkness.

We had different IR and Full-Spectrum camcorders with us as we walked around investigating and exploring most of the old fort property. At one point, two investigators both at the same time saw a shadow person stick its head out from behind a wall, look at us, and then go back. I know both investigators saw it because they both jumped at the same time and made the very same remark at the same time about seeing it. We ran as fast as we could with our camcorders trying to capture it on video and figure out what exactly it was, but it had vanished as quickly as it had appeared to us. We also captured a very strange noise on the camcorders at the very same moment that none of us made......like a spirit was responding to the situation.

The moment of surprise and seeing that shadow person were all captured on our video camcorders and we have the video on the internet again as to our YouTube paranormal channel as to watching and seeing it. We have many of our very good paranormal evidence videos on that paranormal channel "Seeking The Real Paranormal Truth....." and anyone would enjoy seeing what we experienced.

Not everyone in our group that night in the fort had paranormal experiences, which is normal. This is because the paranormal ghostly world does not happen to everyone at the same time and it always seems to happen to paranormal investigators/researchers by extreme surprise. Those moments always make us jump. Do we get afraid sometimes when we encounter scary extreme paranormal activity? Yes, sure we do. Another really good paranormal experience happened later that night while I and my wife Connie were in one of the old elementary school buildings that also used to be one of the old soldier barracks in its day.

This building was not being used anymore by the school district, and there were a lot of things still in the building because they were using it for storage. I believe this was building #2 that we were in at the time, and it was dark and creepy feeling in there. It was also a very large building and there was for sure only myself, my wife Connie, and possibly some ghosts in there with us. I say this jokingly now because the experiences myself and my wife Connie had in there definitely seemed and appeared to be genuine paranormal activity. We were in the hallway looking at things when we heard movement noise down the hallway. I turned the full-spectrum camcorder down that hallway several times trying to see if it would pick up on anything.

As I pointed that camcorder, we both could hear what sounded like a shuffle noise and we also heard the hum or moan of what sounded like a little girl. This moan was captured quite clearly on our digital audio recorder even though the microphone on the camcorder was not strong to pick up. At another point my wife Connie said, "We are not students, we are here to see you". At this moment on our digital audio recorder, right after she said that statement, we picked up a very clear Class A ghostly EVP of a little girl saying the word "Yes" in direct reply to Connie. This really amazed us. We also picked up other very great class A EVP's once we got back home and reviewed all of our equipment for confirmed paranormal activity ghostly evidence.

One of our investigators/researchers, Javier (Harvey) Martinez picked up another very clear eerie sounding Class A EVP of a ghostly woman at one point of their investigation in the fort saying "Hey You!" as if this spirit were trying to get his attention. This again was a very amazing ghostly EVP. We also captured others. We had one of what sounded like a male soldier answering us while walking outside in the night air on the sidewalk talking. The voice was very low and gruff sounding; we knew for sure that it did not match the voices at all of the investigators present. Those ghostly EVP's, a lot of them Class A very clear recordings, were simply not made by us and came from another place. That place that so many of us label either the supernatural or paranormal world.

Our team group had a great time investigating Fort Ringgold as to its charm, history, and paranormal activity. Did we by chance see the ghostly apparition of General Robert E. Lee himself? No, can't say we did on this investigation, but who knows if we ever go back to investigate this old fort again. With the paranormal evidence we collected and confirmed, we know for sure that there was something else happening sometimes on the grounds of that fort.

Some people including some security guards witness soldiers and troops at night formed on the old center parade formation area in the fort. The ghostly apparitions seem and appear possibly to be history mixing with present times, or quite possibly it is so much more as to the true ghosts of Fort Ringgold. Do we think that Fort Ringgold is haunted? Can't say for sure, but we can say that there is a lot of very good paranormal activity that takes place, and the fort definitely in our opinion fits the definition of what haunted means. Our paranormal investigation group had so many very strange unnatural unexplainable things happen to us. If you ever happen to drive through Rio Grande City, Texas and pass this old fort, make sure you take a good look. You just might happen to see the ghostly apparitions of General Robert E. Lee and his troops looking right back at you through history.

Chapter 10: Grey Moss Inn (Helotes, Texas)

Photo By: Dan LaFave

The last chapter included here for all special Texas paranormal purposes is a place that both I and my wife Connie really enjoyed while we were paranormal investigators on another Texas paranormal team years back. We had the pleasure of investigating and researching the historic Grey Moss Inn located at 19010 Scenic Loop Road in Helotes, Texas. This very unique and eloquent restaurant is located not far outside San Antonio, Texas. If you really want to have some great food and possibly have a ghostly encounter at the same time, then this is the restaurant for you to be at. We loved meeting the owner Nell Baeten. She is such a wonderful and nice person, and she has many ghostly stories and history of the Grey Moss Inn to tell you.

Sitting down with Nell, a person immediately feels her warmth and hospitality. She bought the Grey Moss Inn several years back along with her husband Lou by what she told us, and a person can tell that Nell and her husband Lou love the place. It has been their home for years after all. We unfortunately did not get to meet her husband Lou in person, but Nell did tell us about Lou. I believe he was tired and not feeling well the night of the investigation. We heard many stories about reported ghostly happenings at the Grey Moss Inn and wanted to see for ourselves as to these many stories and if those stories and encounters by people were true. Some of these ghostly stories had to do with long ago Indians who used to live on that land where the Grey Moss Inn sits.

There is a huge very old oak tree next to the restaurant called the "Treaty Tree" where it is said that Indians long ago came together as to forming peaceful treaties and other things. It was a social gathering place for the Indians because they all felt the strong spiritual energy that came from this tree. As Nell told us about encounters and things people had seen by that tree, I personally found it all very fascinating. The inn is also said to be the oldest restaurant continuously operating in the Central Texas region. Mary Howell founded the inn in 1929 and it is said that she could really cook well. Nell said that it appeared that Mary had many very good recipes for things. It is said that Mary's ghost still inhabits the Grey Moss Inn to this day. Why are ghosts present in some locations and not in any other locations? In the case of Mary's ghost and spirit, it could very well be because she just loved the place so much, that she just can't leave. Maybe she does not want to leave.

Nell told us that people coming to the restaurant and inn would really enjoy the food. Nell was right, because she provided a meal to us personally, and that meal was just exquisite and good. Myself and my wife Connie could not thank Nell enough for that great hospitality and meal later when we all went back to do the paranormal reveal with her and film some other things. We all made very good videos of that investigation while on that other team After Dark Paranormal Research of Texas, and these videos are on the internet.

That paranormal team I was told is no longer in existence as of last year for reasons, but we still do keep in touch and investigate from time to time with our very good friend who was the actual founder of that Texas team, Eddie Hill. I was a lead investigator on that team. My wife Connie was a researcher as well as investigator. This again was approximately 7 years ago that we commenced this nightly paranormal investigation at the Grey Moss Inn while on that team. People while eating in the great restaurant or walking the grounds of the inn would definitely have ghostly paranormal experiences as to being watched, being touched, hearing strange things, and sometimes seeing ghostly apparitions. The list of paranormal things was long.

As we investigated that night, the whole paranormal group was very excited and looking carefully for anything strange or paranormal. We examined things as we walked around the whole property and the restaurant.

Photo By: Dan LaFave (Myself & My Wife Connie -Taken at the Grey Moss Inn)

At first nothing was happening, and then as it got later, the paranormal group including me started to experience what we thought were paranormal things. At one point, we were walking past the wine storage area. At that precise moment we heard some movement inside there and heard a wine bottle hit the floor and roll towards the storage door. Now, some people might try to say that was natural. We know for a fact that it was not just by the way that it occurred and sounded to us. It was one of those things where you just had to be there to experience that very strange event. When we looked inside, there were no wine bottles on the floor even though we had heard that bottle quite clearly rolling across the floor.

We were also told that there was strong paranormal activity that happened in the women's bathroom of the restaurant. People would be in there and they would hear very strange noises and voices calling out to them. When any male staff after closing would go in there to clean it, they would really encounter strange things. Some male staff would not want to do the cleaning at night in that bathroom. It is said that the ghostly spirit may be Mary and she really hates it when men are in that bathroom. There is a back area of the actual restaurant that looks very romantic, some people while sitting back there have experienced ghostly feelings of being watching, but not in any hostile fashion or anything. Perhaps it again is just the ghost of Mary watching to make sure they are enjoying their food and the elegance of the restaurant and inn.

Our paranormal investigation group did acquire very good clear ghostly EVP's and also strange video evidence of things. We all knew for sure that these very strange events were not natural and they definitely were not explainable with any logic. We simply labeled the very strange things paranormal after we concluded our careful review of everything as to that investigation and did the sit down reveal with Nell to show her what we got and see what her opinion was.

When Nell heard and saw our paranormal evidence, she did not seem surprised because she and many other people already know that the Grey Moss Inn is haunted by more than one spirit at times from all their experiences and encounters. She was excited that we as a paranormal team had confirmed the paranormal activity was indeed real by the collected evidence. A person never truly knows when a ghostly paranormal encounter will happen there.

Nell Baeten is perfectly okay with everything and loves the fact that paranormal activity is there. There are also many people who have had ghostly experiences that also enjoy the Grey Moss Inn for its great food and ghostly happenings. And yes, my wife Connie and I in our own personal opinion as experienced paranormal investigators/researchers do consider the Grey Moss Inn in Helotes, Texas to be haunted. We had a great time there and loved meeting Nell. We could feel both her and her husband's hearts. The ghostly paranormal activity happens there often. There are also the many unexplained unnatural encounters by other people to think otherwise. If driving by Helotes or in Central Texas, be sure to pay a visit to Nell and Lou Baeten and the haunted Grey Moss Inn. It is very romantic and historic as well. If you are looking to have a charming good dinner and some haunting ghostly activity to go along with dinner, then this is the place for you.

Chapter 11: San Juan Hotel (San Juan, Texas)

Photo By: Dan LaFave

When we talk about possible haunted locations, we never quite realize where they may be and what might actually be happening within these places. A lot of times there are many stories or what we may call urban legends about locations and people never quite know if the haunted stories are true or not. This was the situation towards the end of January 2013 when I, my wife Connie, and our investigative group of Javier (Harvey) Martinez, Juan Carlos (J.C.) Cortez Jr., and Edward De La Rosa decided to go in exploring to see what we might encounter or see in this historic hotel. This hotel is located in San Juan in the Texas Rio Grande Valley of deep South Texas not far from the U.S. - Mexico border. There were many stories and rumors of strong haunted ghostly paranormal activity witnessed by both regular people and also paranormal teams before over a span of several years. I had done a lot of research on this hotel since we relocated to the Texas Rio Grande Valley in 2008, but we had never actually had the opportunity to see this old hotel for ourselves.

I was actually thinking to myself that this might be a wasted investigation because the videos I had seen on YouTube and other places on the internet were not that good and really did not depict any real solid ghostly paranormal evidence. I did, however, see many written witness accounts from people describing what they had seen or experienced and there were stories of people who were murdered in this hotel that was established and built in the 1920's. We had contacted the present owner of the hotel to see if there was any possibility of us going in for a controlled paranormal investigation.

The present owner of this old hotel property not only granted us full permission to come in, but he also provided us with a historical detail account of the hotel before he owned it and the name of a past hotel owner Edna Nelson who was shot and murdered along with another innocent bystander/shoe salesman in the lobby of this hotel by the front desk area. The present owner also had heard all the stories of ghostly activity in the hotel and was curious to see what we might find. This shooting was committed by a gunman possibly on the run from the law and it is believed that Edna recognized him when he tried to check into the hotel. This occurred in the early 1940's and information is missing, but Edna was standing in the office booth area and the shoe salesman was in the lobby. It appears that the shoe salesman was killed for being a witness and gunman headed to Mexico. When we read the history and murder accounts of these two people, we were very interested but also skeptical as to what we would actually encounter. We again are very balanced people and investigators as to what we see, a lot of this coming from our past military service or other professional careers we have had. A serious experienced paranormal investigator brings many qualities and views together in drawing a conclusive perspective if a location is haunted or not.

Photo By: Dan LaFave

Upon arriving at the hotel around 7 pm, it was already dark when we got there. The hotel was definitely very spooky looking at night. This hotel property also has over time become a victim of youths vandalizing it by breaking things like windows and spraying graffiti on the walls and also some homeless people actually setting up inside. We also realized then that this hotel is pretty close to a major roadway there in San Juan with modern businesses around it as well. As we stood in front of the hotel looking at it and taking pictures and video of the front and sides, we wondered what exactly was inside. I had a personal ominous feeling of tension that I could not exactly put my finger on at the time.

I told our group that in order for us to have a good controlled investigation this night, that we all had to split up and police/check out this rather large location pretty good to make sure there were no homeless people or others inside or on the property. We also had to make sure that no hazards were inside where we could get hurt walking around. I could tell that this all made the team nervous because we were not totally sure who or what we would encounter inside with its many very dark rooms and areas both upstairs and downstairs. This old hotel now has many boarded up windows and the whole back area and sides are fenced off with barbwire in the present owner trying to keep people out. It is also posted as to trespassing prohibited and that the

San Juan Police Department does patrol and check on this property regularly. We had full written permission legally to be there that night, but were wondering also if the police might show up while we were investigating and exploring.

For this investigation due to fact that there were no power sources on the property, we decided that we would do this investigation pretty much by old school methods. We had several video cameras with us both infrared and full-spectrum and we filmed in such a way that anyone watching would really get an idea of what we were experiencing as we explored this very dark and eerie hotel. The stories and strong rumors we had heard and read about were that a woman, possibly a prostitute, had late one night been attacked by someone. This sounds like many stories heard except for one thing.

The way this young woman was killed it is said was in a very brutal fashion. It is said that she was trying to get out of a top corner upstairs room and was stabbed viciously many times in the back as she screamed several times for help. The murder weapon is not known, nor was there any actual police report to review as to this incident, but the strong rumors are there in saying this story really happened and was covered up possibly. People have said that they can still hear this woman's ear piercing screams and the ghostly apparition of a woman is seen on the 2nd floor of this old hotel walking around. Sometimes people happen to be outside and look up and see a scary looking woman just standing there watching them to only vanish from sight. It is also said that a man hung himself by suicide in one of the rooms. The main story however has to do with the true murders that occurred to the past female owner and shoe salesman. People hear loud voices as if someone is speaking to them, hear loud footsteps and other noises, and see ghostly apparitions and what appear to be shadows moving quickly past them. Some people are actually touched or grabbed by unseen ghostly forces.

As we split up and walked and checked all the many very dark walkways and rooms of this old hotel, I was thinking about all these ghostly stories and wondering again if there were actually any truths to any of it When we explore any ghostly location, we are very balanced as to seeing what we actually find or discover. We do take any written or verbal witness accounts seriously, but we always want to see what we actually see. To us, any paranormal investigation may turn up nothing or all hell could break loose with ghostly things which does sometimes happen to us. Once we all had thoroughly walked this hotel property ensuring that we were alone, we started getting out our equipment and determined how we were going to proceed.

Some of us split up, and were taking pictures and getting video shots of different areas of the hotel. While this happened, different people in our group suddenly started saying they were seeing things moving about. First it was my wife Connie, who said that she was by the old well area when she had seen a dark shadowy figure moving very quickly in an area where none of us was. She immediately went to see, and there was nothing there. She said that this shadowy figure was small and short like a child and was pretty clear to her at the time. Edward De La Rosa had also seen a dark figure standing in one of the walkway areas staring before it disappeared. He described it as a woman wearing a coat and a hat. While I was walking around getting B Roll video footage of areas, I had two occasions where a solid shadow moved very quickly towards me from around a corner and at another point passed right in front of me. I did see this very clearly, but it moved too fast to get a clear image of what I was actually seeing. We were all saying how strange all of this was considering we had just begun our investigation.

My wife Connie had taken many full-spectrum camera pictures and was reviewing all the pictures on her camera when she called me over to look. She said that she could not believe what she had just gotten in one of her pictures.

Photo By: Connie LaFave (Ghostly Shadow Figure)

When she had snapped the pictures, she was taking many pictures simultaneously of the same areas with flash on the camera. She also was looking at these areas for several minutes with her naked eye and was sure that none of us were in these areas when she snapped her pictures. This very authentic ghostly shadow figure picture was captured as she was standing in the back courtyard area of the hotel. She was shooting across the courtyard into the area which strangely enough was near the same well spot where she had previously seen the other shadow figure. We stood for several minutes looking at this amazing picture and also realized that all the pictures were very clear and nothing at all like this was in either the pictures right before or after this picture was obtained. In looking closely at this picture, you can see that it appears to be standing in the open doorway illuminated and is looking back at her.

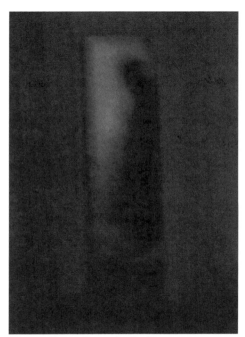

Photo By: Connie LaFave

It was truly a pretty spooky looking picture and we looked at this for several minutes in sheer amazement. We also wondered what else was going to happen and what else we would encounter that night.

I am sure we all had the same feeling of excitement but also tension of being followed or even possibly stalked by something unseen. That hotel suddenly became a lot darker and ominous feeling. I decided that we would all run group EVP sessions in different parts of the hotel with different people and that we would ask clever and unique questions as to seeing what responses we would get. We were not in this hotel to just confirm if there was paranormal activity, but also to see if we would get intelligent answers to our questions on when, where, or how things happened to these people from the past who were killed or died in this hotel. As many years as our whole group has been researching the ghostly paranormal world, we are interested more in getting higher level evidence than just confirming if ghostly activity possibly exists. We are on the level where we want and usually do establish some higher level of intelligent response communication. It is amazing sometimes what the dead have to say.

Photo By: Connie LaFave

As we conducted our recorded EVP sessions, we were all hearing very strange things and movements around and above us. At one point, I was filming in a room area to the left of the main hotel lobby and I suddenly heard very loud boot walking sounds right above me. I called out to the group saying that I heard something and one of the members Harvey exclaimed that he had also just seen another shadow figure moving really fast near my area. He and I both said our experiences at exactly the same time and both seemed to be directly related due to fact that we both experienced at the same moment.

As we went all around the hotel to different rooms both upstairs and downstairs, we were interested in trying to find out what room the stabbing death might have occurred. We had gone into several upstairs rooms recording EVP sessions. It was during this time that we all suddenly hearing voices saying things out loud in response to our questions. At one point which is also clearly heard on our posted YouTube video of this investigation, a man says very clearly in a creepy and ominous voice "Jesus Is Not Here" when we were again asking as to if this was the room where the woman was attacked and what happened to her. We even heard a female voice say something to us in this room even though my wife was the only female present and she was downstairs at this time and far away.

There even is a downstairs small basement area of this hotel that is pretty spooky and creepy. When walking down those side stairs, a person almost feels like they are entering a cave system or something. When we did our exploring down there, we all had very strange feelings of being watched. There were times where each of us found ourselves turning around as the night progressed because we felt there was someone moving behind us. When we turned around, of course there was no one there. The most dramatic and scary moment of this investigation occurred when we went to the last upstairs corner room area of this old hotel. For some reason, we had all avoided going into this room up till now. We had all made comments that this room gave us the creeps. It felt as if something was trying to draw us into it. Earlier that night, we had also asked in the lobby during an EVP recording session if the murdered Edna Nelson was there with us. It was heard on our digital audio recorder at that moment what sounded like a woman walking up to us and then saying yes.

As we all walked into that last upstairs corner room, it seemed very different to us. For one thing, all the rooms in this hotel had very solid concrete brick walls and our voices echoed in all of the previous rooms we did recording sessions in. For some strange reason, this last upstairs room had no echo to it even though it was constructed the same as the other rooms. There also was a very eerie chill that we all felt as we walked into this room to set up for our last EVP recording session of the investigation that night. I could see that we were all feeling strange things in that room, all of us were constantly turning around and hearing strange movement noises in that scary feeling room. In the paranormal world, there are moments when paranormal researchers feel on guard as to something bad possibly happening and this was one of those moments we were anticipating at the time. As we started, that was when the problems began.

The first problem was that some of our equipment started malfunctioning as to battery drainage problems. We were losing some various pieces of equipment to this. Some people would say this is natural, but we know otherwise. Something very ominous was in that room draining our batteries and we had the feeling that we were about to be attacked by something. It was later heard on our digital audio recorders which are again on our complete YouTube investigation video as to the different very loud and clear ominous voices heard. The ghostly voices sound as if several spirits were in that room with us and were battling each other or possibly us. Those recordings are very creepy sounding. During our recording session, I found myself turning and looking behind me. I had the very distinct feeling that someone was standing behind me and felt touches as if by fingers at times. It was then that I felt it, the worst pain I have ever felt during an investigation before. Something had just stabbed my lower right side.

The initial pain was deep and very excruciating as I suddenly bent over from the pain. The rest of the group screamed out to me but could see the pain in my eyes. They could tell that something very bad had just occurred to me. What I felt was like a seven to eight inch ice pick being stabbed into my lower back side and I could even feel it internally as if it had penetrated a kidney or something. The strange thing of course is the fact that this was a paranormal event and there was a red mark where I was feeling the pain, but of course no actual wound. What I was feeling was that stabbing pain possibly as to what the woman had felt when she was stabbed and being killed. This also was just one stab penetration that I was feeling and it was the worst pain I had ever felt. I doubled over for several minutes and was thinking to myself at that time if this was only one stabbing action.......what did the many stabbing wounds feel like for that woman? I also had the feeling that she was reaching out to me in trying to show me what it was like.

The rest of the group in the room with me was worried and said that we should go. I found myself bent over and limping in pain as we walked back down the hallway and then down the main stairs to the hotel lobby area where my wife Connie was. My wife could see how much pain I was in as she examined my lower right back area carefully. My thought at that moment was that we had found what we were looking for. We had found that confirmation of those ghostly stories and rumors we had heard about from other people. My thought at that moment was that we were done and it was time to go. I was having a hard time handling that stabbing pain. We all had distressed looks on our faces at that time from everything experienced that night at the old San Juan Hotel. We had experienced so many very strange ghostly things that night. We were certain in our minds that this old hotel is indeed haunted by something quite ominous. We also had the feelings that very bad things did indeed happen in the past to people. We could not wait to pack up our equipment and head home. We also later could not believe the amazing clear, loud, and ominous ghostly EVP's we had all acquired on our digital audio recorders.

There were not just a few EVP's, but many of them. We also could easily see that these EVP's were not caused by any natural means. It was clear that they were reaching out to us. The dead spirits that now inhabit that old hotel property. We were convinced that the stories told by people are true, because the evidence of what we acquired proved to us that there are many ghostly things occurring in the hotel. A week after the investigation after everything was looked at and examined; all I could think of were all those creepy moments walking the grounds of this historic hotel. Yes, it is true that this hotel is now abandoned and in a great state of disrepair and vandalism, but it was also clear to us that the ghosts are present and that the San Juan Hotel is indeed very haunted.

Picture By: Javier (Harvey) Martinez

Chapter 12: Gonzales County Jail
(Gonzales, Texas Old Jail Museum)

Photo By: Javier (Harvey) Martinez

I talk with many other paranormal teams, especially in Texas as to places they have been to, investigated before, and what they found. When a very serious paranormal investigator has been exploring and investigating the paranormal over the span of several years like I have, a person hears of several locations with possible haunted activity within them. Some stories are mixed as to what different people hear, encounter, or get as to paranormal evidence. Some people have extreme things occur and other people do not feel or encounter anything. This is why the ghostly paranormal world is so mysterious because of the fact that things do not happen to everyone exactly the same way each time. For me, my wife Connie, and other people we have investigated with before, we can definitely say this is the case most of the time. This is why again that we like to draw our own personal perspective as to if a location has possible haunted ghostly activity happening or not. We have to have really scary experiences and have gotten a lot of confirmed paranormal activity evidence before we would label any place as being haunted in the meaning of this word.

When I first heard about ghostly things happening at the old historic Gonzales County Jail (Old Jail Museum) located in Gonzales, Texas I was more than curious. This was several years ago that I started hearing things from various both paranormal or just regular people as to things they encountered while either investigating or just simply touring this old historic jail during the day. There was something about this old historic Texas jail that really intrigued me. Maybe it had to do with the fact that people were really executed by somewhat brutal means inside this Texas jail long ago by hanging on the gallows. Maybe it had to due with the fact that this historic jail just simply looked scary both outside and inside. When I asked our investigative group of my wife Connie, Javier (Harvey) Martinez, Juan Carlos (J.C.) Cortez Jr., and Edward De La Rosa what they thought as to what they saw or heard about as to this old jail, we all were very intrigued and fascinated to see what we would actually find during a controlled paranormal investigation into the night.

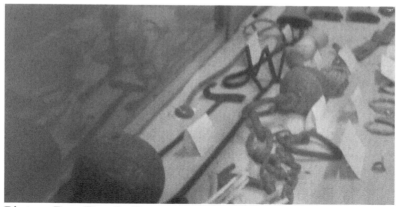

Picture By: Dan LaFave

After we set everything up with the management of the historic Gonzales Jail Museum as to a controlled nightly paranormal investigation, we headed out one Saturday afternoon in February 2013 for the 4 1/2 hour Texas road trip. When we arrived and got out of the vehicle, we were really struck by how old and ominous this huge old historic jail structure is. The pictures do not really do this place justice in giving the feeling that we had. This old jail sits nearly in the middle of Gonzales, Texas which is a town that has quite a bit of history going back to the days of The Alamo and Texas Independence frontier days. This museum also has very interesting historical artifacts on display to view as to both the notorious criminals and also law people who have been associated with this jail in the past. I noticed when we arrived just how spooky this place was just by looking at the old heavy steel front door leading us inside.

Just a few months before, some paranormal friends and investigators Alejandro Dominguez and Jay Villarreal who we have investigated with before at times in different Texas locations had some very bad things happen to them while investigating and filming inside this historic Texas jail. They had come into this place just like other locations before not really knowing what to expect. During the investigation, they had many disturbing things happen and at one time Jay Villarreal while being filmed on camera was actually severely grabbed and choked by an unseen ghostly force and had to run outside for several minutes before it got better. He and Alejandro Dominquez had been in the Lunatic Room which was a very secured room on the lower level of this old jail where any inmates with severe mental problems were separated from the rest of the inmates. Alejandro Dominguez (The Dead Explorer) and Jay Villarreal were just conducting an EVP session and filming when this hostile event occurred and this video can be seen on The Dead Explorer YouTube video channel as to what happened in detail. We also have our complete video of our investigation in this old jail on our YouTube channel Seeking The Real Paranormal Truth.

Walking inside the old historic jail, we were given a tour by a member of the museum staff. He told us that both historical things and also ghostly paranormal things that he, other staff members, the public on tours, and other paranormal teams have encountered before. He told us that many people during the day simply coming in to tour the jail encounter sometimes extreme things happening. One of the things he told us was that when any women go up on the 2nd floor into the cells upstairs and close the cell doors, that extreme things sometime happen to them. He said that many women have come down the metal stairs from the cell areas totally freaked out saying that they were either touched, grabbed, or their hair pulled. They also hear voices as if someone calling out to them. They ask him or the museum staff if there was anyone else up there with them and he tells them no, that they were the only people to have gone up the stairs to the other blocked off areas of the old jail.

When he told us this, we could not wait to experiment with a few different things in regards to all of those cell areas of the museum. When we ascended the old metal stairs to get a view of those cell areas and the replication of the old hangman gallows, I could feel the utter creepiness of this place. We were all wide-eyed as we looked at everything.

Dan LaFave (Standing On Hangman Gallows)

The stories are that people hear voices, are touched or grabbed, see ghostly apparitions, and hear footsteps and strange moving noises. We could not wait to get started as we unpacked our equipment and split up into two different groups as to going to different areas of this old jail to explore. Before doing this though, we all went as a group to the Lunatic Room to conduct a thorough controlled EVP recording sessions with various cameras and equipment consisting of digital audio recorders and other devices. The front door was locked and no one else was in this whole jail besides just us and Mr. Hand (museum staff). It was quiet for a little while into our EVP session for a few minutes before we decided to play back what we had just recorded as to our questions on the recorders.

Within just a few minutes we heard a very clear EVP male response saying one of our investigators names and something else in direct response to a question. When we heard this, our ears and senses suddenly tuned in because it was beginning to happen. The ghosts of this old historic jail were just beginning to communicate with us which was just the beginning. A few minutes after that EVP, we captured and heard another very clear and loud ghostly EVP answering my wife Connie directly. It was of a man's voice clearly saying "hurt me"! This paranormal investigation that night was going to get a whole lot more interesting, exciting, and scary before it was over for us. We were excited but also nervous as to what exactly what else we were going to encounter that night. We found ourselves turning around quite a lot thinking we were being watched. We also found ourselves constantly staring at the huge hangman gallows structure and the rope noose hanging from it. We knew from what the museum staff told us that this was a replica of the original hangman gallows' structure that was torn down in the the 1950's, but this thing was still very scary looking.....especially in the pitch dark that we were exploring in at the time with our equipment and eyes. The hangman gallows stood right in front of us as to its scary and ominous sight.

Photo By: Dan LaFave (Connie LaFave touching noose)

It was in the Lunatic Room with its big and heavy iron door that our friends and fellow Texas paranormal researchers and explorers Jay Villarreal and Alejandro Dominguez (aka The Dead Explorer) had their very extreme and violent paranormal experience and encounter a few weeks before we arrived for our exploration of this old jail. They had been filming and conducting an EVP session in the Lunatic Room and they both said that they started to feel really strange in that room, but carried on. Jay Villarreal started to on film become very agitated as to the questions he was asking during their EVP recording session and appeared to become flustered and started to deliver more direct provoking questions as if in anger. Alejandro later said that he could feel this and he himself felt as if something bad were going to happen, but he was unclear what. At one point, Jay touched his throat and said that something or someone was trying to strangle and choke him. His eyes became bloodshot and watery as he fought to just try to talk and signal to Alejandro who was filming as to what was happening to him. Jay just turned and yelled that he had to get out of there and outside of the building and they both ran outside. Once outside, Alejandro continued to film and captured very clearly as to the expression on Jay's face and his bodily mannerisms and gestures that he was indeed being choked by something previously in that room. He was still suffering the effects of this quite clearly and could barely speak outside. If you want to see this video, just be sure to go to The Dead Explorer YouTube video channel page and look for the video labeled attacked in Texas jail. You will be able to see.

When I had talked with them previously about their extreme experience, I wanted them to actually go back to this historic Texas jail with us together to see what might happen again. Jay Villarreal at the last minute suddenly became sick and could not make the trip to Gonzales, Texas, but Alejandro Dominguez was able to join up with us to explore this historic jail/prison again throughout the night. He arrived later that night after we had already begun exploring, but we along with him did encounter and have more very strange what we label paranormal and possibly haunted paranormal experiences. I will let you know in detail towards the end of this chapter what actually happened to Alejandro Dominguez towards the end of our nightly investigation, it was very strange and scary looking especially in the dark.

Many people ask serious paranormal researchers why it is we always investigate in the dark and why we use video cameras with the capability of seeing in the dark either by infrared or full-spectrum means. The answer to this question is always very simple and direct, because there is a main reason why we do this. Ghostly paranormal activity whether that be somewhat normal or even possibly a lot more extreme to be labeled in the haunted category can and usually does occur during either the day or night. It really does not matter and happens to people at all times of the day. A person would be surprised. If you ever talk sincerely with someone who lives or works in a haunted location that is very active, they will tell you all of their stories and you will be very intrigued to say the least. We as paranormal researchers and explorers do most of what we do at night simply because the whole world is a lot quieter at night and much easier to determine what may actually be paranormal versus normal as to sounds and other things. We also tend to capture better possible evidence by means of the dark because our cameras that see in the dark as to different spectrums are more likely to pick things up that the human eye cannot see due to limitations. The video cameras that we use can see a much broader spectrum of visible light than the human eye can.

While back in the Lunatic Room, we were hearing very strange things as to we went through a few recording sessions. We were also at times seeing strange things with our eyes as to shadow movement that was not caused by our own movement or forms. While in the Lunatic Room, we basically were standing in a circle pattern and Mr. Hand who was with the museum staff was with us.

Photo By: Dan LaFave (Of Connie LaFave in Lunatic Rm.)

It was very spooky in this room to say the least and we were all standing in this room, but could at the same time hear movement and footstep sounds coming from the hallway outside and other parts of the old building. This place echoed due to all the iron and concrete, it was easy to tell when we were actually hearing an audible ghostly foot step or voice responding to our questions.

As we continued to ask questions, our whole group was becoming more intrigued as time went on as to what we were hearing and experiencing. This whole historic jail/prison seemed to be opening up to us as to its ghostly happenings. We were clearly becoming alarmed as time went on as to what was occurring.

Photo By: Dan LaFave (Of Harvey Martinez)

As our recording session went on in the Lunatic Room, we could not wait to get up on the second floor as to the old cell areas. We were hearing lots of things up there, and I even heard at one time someone ascending the old steel steps leading up there even though no one else was in the building. No one else that is besides the ghosts.

Once we got up into the cell areas, we started to experience and hear even more things that seemed far from natural. We were hearing cell doors closing loudly and actual audible voices calling out to us at times. Once we entered the cells, we started to feel very strange as if some kind of energy existed in there with us. Can safely say that we all agreed this was not a good energy either. It seemed as if someone or something was just waiting to pounce on us at any moment. It was not a good feeling at all; we even became slightly nauseated feeling at times. We were filming this whole investigation and this video and whole exploration can be found on our YouTube video channel "Seeking The Real Paranormal Truth".

Picture of Dan LaFave in old jail/prison cell

We were hearing things and checking them out, it was easy to see that everyone was encountering very strange things. It is hard to describe, but this historic jail/prison is just very creepy inside. It is also unique as to its history and events that took place there, but a person when walking around just feels things, especially if that person is alone. We found that we just kept turning around or looking into different cell areas because we could hear what sounded like other people in those areas. We were becoming agitated by what we were encountering and again felt like we might get jumped by something at any moment. That is a very uneasy feeling for any experienced paranormal researcher or investigator to have because that feeling does not come often. When it does come, it can literally put one of us on edge and alarm as to something very extreme and strange happening which is usually the case when we feel these kinds of things in locations.

Photo By: Dan LaFave (Of Connie LaFave)

At one point, I decided to put my wife Connie LaFave in a cell by herself to see what would happen to her. As we closed the cell door, we never had any idea what would be captured at that moment by our digital audio recorders. We captured a very ominous male voice saying something just as the cell door was being closed with her inside. A few seconds after this, she asks a question and another ominous scary sounding male voice says clearly "Be Quiet" and then the voice of what sounds like a male child says "Grab Her" very loudly on the recorder. We could not hear this at the time but we did hear what sounded like footsteps both behind and above the jail cells we were in. We could hear what clearly sounded like some people moving about unseen. Even though we were nervous while conducting this paranormal experiment, later upon hearing these ghostly EVP clear voices, this made us even more intrigued and nervous about everything encountered during exploration that night.

I have to admit that the energy felt in this historic jail as the night's exploration wore on really surprised me. My excitement and anticipation was at the highest levels it had been in a long time. I along with my wife Connie and our paranormal friends and explorers were really feeling things and this was much more than just general feelings. Just about everyone was walking around wide-eyed within the confines of this very dark historic jail. It was said that even though the hangman gallows was a replica of the one tore down in the 1950's, that this is how it looked. We were also told that somewhere in the ceiling structure was an old hook where the rope was run through as to executing the prisoners. The last Texas prisoner was executed in this old jail in the early 1900's and many prisoners could hear the old clock on the courthouse next to the jail as it chimed away their fate. There were six legal hangings that took place in Gonzales, with the first in 1855. In 1878, it was estimated that approximately 4,000 people arrived to witness the human suffering and shedding of blood of Brown Bowen. Another hanging took place in 1881. After this jail was built, the first permanent gallows were built in 1891 and Albert Howard's hanging occurred on March 18, 1921 where he professed his innocence. There were also a few times when the person hung did not actually die the first time and had to be hung again. A lot of this could easily tie into all the paranormal haunted happenings taking place within the confines of this historic jail.

When our good friend Alejandro Dominguez has his extreme event occur at the end of the night, we were in the process of wrapping up our investigation. He had taken off to film himself and asked that a member of our investigative group close the old iron heavy door to the Lunatic Room where he was at creating a locked in atmosphere. He did not realize that our investigative member had actually truly latched and locked that heavy door where he could not get out even if he wanted to. Things started to happen to him in there as he asked questions while filming. He felt a very strange presence in one of the corners that had scratching on the wall as if someone sat there and continually scratched their nails on the concrete wall. I along with another member of our group realized that he was gone and we went down to this room to see how he was doing because it was eerily quiet in that room all of a sudden. We unlatched the door and went in to find him sitting in the corner of the room in a trance-like state.

He was not acting the same and just staring off into blank space. We took his video camera from him and started to film him sitting there. After a few minutes, he quit talking and just sat there staring. Even his face seemed to change because at that moment, it did not look like him. He then said some strange things that did not make any sense. When we asked again if he was alright, he suddenly snapped out of his trance-like state and looked up at us asking what happened. It was found that he did not even remember doing what he did. His last words or thoughts were that he felt strange as if he could feel the pain and visions of the long ago mentally affected prisoner who sat on the floor in that corner, possibly in a straight jacket. It was around this moment, that the whole room became engulfed with a strong medicine smell as of an old ointment from the 1800's or early 1900's, the smell permeated the room and our nostrils and then vanished as quickly as it had manifested.

We packed up our equipment and said goodbye to Mr. Hand and took a last look at this historic jail/prison that we would label as being haunted from our extreme experiences and the compelling paranormal activity evidence that was later found by us there. All of this information was compiled into a video that is on our YouTube video channel "Seeking The Real Paranormal Truth".

Photo By: Javier Martinez

Hope that you have enjoyed all the stories and real sometimes extreme ghostly encounters that I have personally experienced for many years in Texas and other states. Texas again is full of rich history, heritage, and ghostly paranormal activity. The old west of Texas and other states is alive as well. I personally think the old west is trying to yell out to us through history. The ghosts of that sometimes brutal old west are possibly reaching out. Could they be telling their story? The best haunting ghost stories are the ones that are lived and experienced.

All that we see or seem is but a dream within a dream....

Quote: Edgar Allan Poe

15855450R00113

Made in the USA
San Bernardino, CA
09 October 2014